Soap Making Business Startup

The Ultimate Guide to Make Natural and Organic Soap at Home

Floy Sweeney

© Copyright

All rights reserved

This book is targeted towards offering essential details about the subject covered. The publication is being provided with the thought that the publisher is not mandated to render an accounting or other qualified services. If recommendations are needed, professional or legal, a practiced person in the profession ought to be engaged.

In no way is it legal to recreate, duplicate, or transfer any part of this document in either electronic means or printed format. Copying of this publication is strictly prohibited, and its storage is not allowed unless with written authorization from the publisher. All rights reserved.

The information supplied herein is specified to be honest because any liability in regards to inattention or otherwise, by any use or abuse of any directions, processes, or policies confined within is the sole and utter obligation of the recipient reader. Under no circumstances will any form of legal duty or blame be held against the publisher for any reparation, damages, or financial loss because of the information contained herein. The author owns the entire copyrights not maintained by the publisher.

The information stated herein is provided for educational purposes exclusively. The presentation of the data is without contractual agreement or any kind of warranty assurance.

All trademarks inside this book are for clarifying purposes only and are possessed by the owners themselves, not allied with this document.

Disclaimer

All erudition supplied in this book is specified for educational and academic purposes only. The author is not in any way to be responsible for any outcomes that emerge from using this book. Constructive efforts have been made to render information that is both precise and effective. Still, the author is not to be held answerable for the accuracy or use/misuse of this information.

Foreword

I will like to thank you for taking the very first step of trusting me and deciding to purchase/read this life-transforming book. Thanks for investing your time and resources on this product.

I can assure you of precise outcomes if you will diligently follow the specific blueprint I lay bare in the information handbook you are currently checking out. It has transformed lives, and I firmly believe it will equally change your own life too.

All the information I provided in this Do It Yourself piece is easy to absorb and practice.

INTRODUCTION

Soap is among the many original items in our lives. For many of us in the western world, we make use of soap daily. We use it to cleanse our bodies, our homes, and our clothing, and when the soap is remarkable, it can purify and wash on a psychological or even spiritual level too. On how many occasions have you roamed the aisles of a shop pondering over bottles of body cleansers and bars of soaps, wishing you could find one that was genuinely different and fit just for you? Or probably you have visited smaller artisan markets where soap makers showed their magnificently wholesome-looking soap, and you questioned if it were possible to make soap yourself. The fact is that yes, you can make those soaps yourself, and you can tailor them to your needs and wants, and the process isn't complicated at all. Lots of people feel slightly frightened by soap, making the feeling that the equipment, chemicals, and time involved or required for the process make it something that they are better off avoiding.

The truth is that soap making is quite easy, and people have securely and successfully been making soap throughout history. It is thought that the very first soap makers were the Babylonians, with evidence of the first set of soaps being produced as early as 2800 B.C. Those earlier soaps were developed from rich oils combined with ashes. A little later in history, the Egyptians valued soaps crafted from animal fats and alkaline salts that they used to clean their bodies. From there onward, different cultures and civilizations developed unique soap formulas that were used for a range of purposes, from routine spiritual practices to the cleaning of wool and textiles. They were even used medicinally as we moved to modern times. What is intriguing about soaps, like so many other things in history, is that each of these individual cultures discovered that blending oils and fats with substances such as ash, alkaline salts, and other active ingredients produced a compound that had value in cleaning our bodies, belongings, and even souls.

A little history of soap making is essential to understanding not just the need for soap throughout time, but to mention that even more primitive societies (those without the knowledge that we have today, those without the protective equipment, and those without internet to use hundreds of soap-making concepts) in some way managed to not only produce soap but developed it into the product that we are familiar with today.

By embracing this ancient craft of soap-making, you are connecting yourself to history and your traditions. You are also learning a skill that is not just important but very enjoyable.

In this book, you will find all that you need to start making homemade soaps. I aim to simplify the process and help you see how simple homemade soap-making is. There is indeed some form of science and chemistry involved with soap-making, and if you are interested in that aspect of knowledge, I encourage you to explore it more. However, If you do not care about anything related to chemistry, this book is written to make it readable for you. The guidelines are set out for you, together with a terrific set of soap-making formulas that you can co of when you are ready. Soap making is an enjoyable and time-honored craft, one that can become addictive as soon as you start.

Now that you have what you require, there is no reason to wait any longer. It's time to put on your rubber gloves, dive in, and experience the enjoyment of home soap making.

Have you ever imagined making your homemade soap? You may be curious about the procedure or feel that store-bought soap and other skincare products are too costly. It might also be that you're stressed over the chemical ingredients in your soap and simply prefer the natural and healthier alternative. In any case, don't worry! This book will take you through the procedure of making your soap at home without any problem.

So, before you question your abilities, feel confident that if you can make chocolate chip cookies, you can make soap! All the tools you need are now products you can find in your home if not at your neighborhood grocery shop! There is little or no difficulty as this book carefully describes in detail the steps in the most convenient possible manner. You'll be blending your ingredients in an average of 30 minutes. Continue reading; you will be happy you did.

CHAPTER ONE

Terminologies in Soap Making

As you begin your homemade soap making journey, there are a variety of terms that you will stumble upon time and time again. A few of these terms are highly standard and distinct, while others have significances specific to the art of soap making. The most common soap making terminologies are listed below:

- **Rebatching:** The treatment of creating a new soap with a grating or shredding a formerly crafted soap, adding a little liquid, and afterward heating until it is smooth enough to put into mold and mildews. It can also be made use of to conserve a batch of soap having an issue or a quantity that did not wind up looking as you prepared.

- **Rendering:** The treatment of melting beef suet or tallow and doing away with all of the meat, other contaminants, and adding a percentage of baking soft drink to get the fat detoxified. This procedure is usually done often to guarantee purity. You can acquire beef fat that is now rendered.

- **Ash:** It refers to the soda ash that gets on the soap as a result of the lye connecting with oxygen throughout the saponification treatment. Every soap has a chance of developing ash. Covering and insulating your soap will decrease the quantity of ash that produces on your soap once it is in the mold.

- Curing: It is the duration after the soap is built and saponified where you allow the soap rest so that excess water can evaporate, generating a more challenging and resilient bar soap.

- Orange Spot: A sign that your soap has actually oxidized and usually spoiled. Orange spots are typical rancidity indicators.

- Saponification: The chemical effect between lye and oils that develops glycerin on your soap's surface area, you can either vapor the soap gently or scrub it off. You may likewise pick to leave the ash on your soap, as it positions no injury to the skin.

- Cold Process: The procedure of making soap via incorporating fats, oils, and lye without actively adding warm to the process. All of the heat is used by the chain reaction that accompanies the addition of lye.

- Lye Discount: When you use less lye than what is generally called for to saponify every bit of the oil present in your formula, this leaves a portion of the oil remaining in its natural state that can be absorbed by the skin. This procedure is also described as "extremely fatting."

- **Lye:** The common name for salt hydroxide. Lye is an essential part of the soap making procedure. It is the blend of lye with oils and water that activates the chain responses that create soap.

- **pH:** The unit dimension of exactly how acidic or fundamental a material is. The pH of your soap will certainly alter throughout the saponification treatment. You prefer your soap to have a pH that continues to be in a neutral degree of 7 to 10.

Tallow: It describes a Rendered beef fat that is taken advantage of as a choice of fat in some soap recipes.

Tracing: A particular point at which soap ends up being thick sufficient to take into the molds. At this stage, the soap has gotten to a consistency where the oils will not revoke it. It is usual to include colorants, scents, and fillers at the tracing point.

- **Molding:** Pouring your soap mixtures after it has traced right into molds that represent the desired final form of the soap.

Saponification Value: (SAP) This is the quantity of lye needed to saponify a specific oil entirely. When creating your soap making solutions, each oil has a particular SAP worth that needs to be well calculated.

Seize: The fast solidification throughout soap making that kinds thick globs of soap, making it unable to be put right into mold and mildews.

Dinner fatting: Have a look at the description of "Lye Discount."

CHAPTER TWO

Soap-Making Essentials

Soap making is more like food preparation, and you may presently have most of the gadgets you will require lying around your residence. When you start using something for soap making, keep it for that to prevent the transfer of essential chemicals and oil to your cooking tools.

Products and Equipment for Homemade Soap

Soap making does not require a good deal of equipment; nevertheless, some products are essential to have before you can also begin.

Stocking your kitchen or workplace with the supplies that you need isn't an exception made facility, along with it doesn't require to damage the financial institution. You likely presently have the bulk of the necessary items in your home. It is needed to keep in mind that when you mark a thing to be used for soap making, that it is forever assigned for soap making. Do not use your grandma's glass gauging cups unless you are that you never wish to make a set of cookies with them ever before again.

Take good care of your soap making devices by maintaining it saved entirely in a good location where it will certainly not get harmed. Regularly tidy your points after usage and before deciding to place them away. The longer you wait to wipe soap deposits, the much more difficult it will certainly be. Always follow any suggestions or directions worrying storage space, use, and maintenance area of your soap making tools.

Below is a checklist of essential products and sorts of devices that you will call for to contend hand throughout the soap-making procedure:

1. Sturdy rubber handwear covers, apron, safety, and security goggles, and long-sleeved tops: this will unquestionably protect the individual from caustic spills in addition to fumes.

2. Vinegar: required to lug hand in all times. It reduces the results of the salt hydroxide (caustic)-- acid neutralizes an antacid-- and also, if you try to get some quantity of caustic soda or raw soap on your skin, a fast spray used by washing will shield against any burn. If, like me, you have children in addition to pet dogs tidying up the floorings and surface with vinegar alleviates any anxiety over unidentified spills.

3. Stainless-steel pan: for making the soap in (3 liters (5¼ pints) minimum). Do not use any kind of other sorts of steel, such as aluminum, as it will positively respond with the soap.

4. Warmth source for melting oil: your hob (range) or a tiny electrical exterior camping stove that can be used anywhere.

5. Mold and mildews: put raw soap right into these to generate the primary form of your final result soaps. There are numerous

types conveniently available, varying from cardboard lined with greaseproof (wax) paper to customized silicone mold and mildews that allow initial soap launch. The best patterns are silicone or durable plastic, which can begreased or lined. If you are an avid recycler, you can use drains pipes, juice boxes, uninhabited cardboard, plastic pots, and also cake molds. Different websites are marketing business molds that enable you to lower constant bars along with unique silicone mold and mildews (see Suppliers). Commonly, the more significant the amount of soap you make at the same time, the better the outcomes. It is attractive to place soap right into rather little silicone-shaped molds; they lost cozy rapidly, and additionally, saponification will take a lot longer.

To create tiny bars, wait up until you make an embedded in a vast mold and stand out the smaller sized frame and mildews in addition to the great pattern before insulation to take advantage of the additional warm produced.

6. Sticking movie (plastic cover) or resilient plastic: for covering the surface area of your molded soap to prevent unsightly soft beverage ash (a white powder that is frequently generated when air reacts with the soap throughout saponification).

Soda ash is not harmful, but a visual problem that can be messed up off.

7. Greaseproof paper: to line cardboard or wood molds.

8. Place two big towels and cardboard: for safeguarding raw soap once it has been poured into a mold and mildew to avoid cozy loss and make certain full saponification.

Place two large towels on your table adhered to by a sheet of cardboard, afterward the soap and likewise another layer of cardboard. Cover the soap in the towels. In a cold space, an added covering can be covered around the soap.

9. Ranges for assessing: exact electronic ranges that go down to 1g (1/16 oz) and up to a minimum of 3kg (6lb 8oz) (If you desire to go right into industrial manufacturing in the future, a collection of professional trade scales will be asked for).

10. Plastic or glass bowls and containers: for considering out sodium hydroxide and dehydrated energetic ingredients, for mixing sodium hydroxide and also for establishing water.

11. Tidy jam (jelly) containers: for saving necessary oils. It is recommended to re-use jam containers for details blends of essential oil as opposed to cleaning the oils in a recipe washer or the sink.

Basic Soap-Making Tools

The following devices are essential in soap making and will be made use of over and over during the process.

1. Soap-making thermometer and jam thermostat: The soap-making thermostat is needed for usage with the caustic fluid as it does not wear off in a salt hydroxide (caustic soda) as a jam thermostat would.

Jam thermostat is, nevertheless, handy for holding on the side of a pan of oil to assess the temperature level.

2. Silicone whisks, spatulas, spoons, and stick blender or mixer (optional):.

These are perfect for usage in soap making as they do not dissolve in acid and cozy combinations. A suitable silicone spatula will certainly also eliminate an unusual amount of soap that would or else be wasted. Whisks are used to mix the raw soap. A stick blender or food processor is far more productive when you are getting proficient in the art of soap making with a whisk and are moving up to bigger batches.

3. Cheese grater: for grating your completed soap to recycle it right into a choice of new items.

4. Silicone or plastic ladle: to place the detergent directly into the molds if the pan is as well hefty to raise when making massive sets.

5. Sharp blade, cheese cutter, soap reducing tool, the cutting board: To cut your soap bars for drying when the soap is ready to reduce.

6. Spray oil or paintbrush for oiling mold and mildews with a spray or thawed out potential.

7. Coffee mill or pestle and additionally mortar for grinding all-natural herbs, spices in addition to oats.

8. PH strips for evaluating your ended up soap once it has cooled down and likewise set.

Affordable litmus papers are comfortably acquired online.

Oils and Fats.

There are lots of oils and fats that can be used in the soap making process. This section of the book will be taking a look at one of the most natural fats, and oils made use of in soap making, their functions, and precisely just how they will boost a bar of soap. The oil and grease used in soapmaking offer numerous services, consisting of figuring out precisely just how much lather your soap creates, how hard the solvent is, and how soothing the last product is.

Emollients: These are the oils that contribute favorably by raising the soap's moisturization. Consider oils such as apricot, avocado, enjoyable almond, and also jojoba, to name a couple of.

Lather-producing fats: If you want a soap with a stable lather, coconut, and castor oil are the two fats that develop one of the most effective latherings. A whole lot much more is not always much better with these two, and a little goes a long way in developing a dense lather. A lot of coconut oil can be excessively cleansing, leading to dry skin, and too much castor oil has the potential of making your soap dry and as well as crumbly. At a point, excessive castor oil begins to get rid of the lathering building of soap rather than adding to it.

Hardeners: Most hardeners are fats that are strong at area temperature. These fats assist in reinforcing along with hardening your soap, prolonging its life. Instances consist of grease (and different other pet dog fats), veggie shortening, and coconut oil. Olive oil does not work as a hardener on its very own; however, it can boost the solidifying capacity of different other oils.

When making, there is an excellent option of fats and also oils to pick from soaps. When starting, you will likely desire to remain with the ones that you are aware of, are sensibly low-cost, and are simple to make use of. Following is a listing of several one of the most effective oils to take into account for beginning and likewise for sophisticated soap making.

Apricot Kernel Oil: This light oil is comparable to pleasant almond oil and is well fit to sensitive skin kinds. It is abundant in vitamins, has a moderate aroma, and is taken in quickly right into the skin.

Argan Oil: Very plentiful in vitamin E and vitamin K. This oil is among the much even more pricey oils that you will discover on the market. For that reason, maybe best to use Argan oil in rebatched, or hand maker made soaps to make sure that you do not shed any massive quantity of the oil with the process of saponification.

Avocado Seed Oil: This type of oil is rich in vitamins A, E, and D, with each other with healthy protein and amino acids. It is a gorgeous addition to include soaps that you plan to have a beautiful hydrating house, primarily because the skin promptly absorbs it.

Babassu Oil: This oil may seem lesser recognized when compared to many of the others that you can find on this checklist, it should have stated because it is a suitable substitute for coconut oil in soaps if you mean to produce a resilient, durable soap. Babassu oil frequently tends to preserve wetness and be much less drying than coconut oil can be.

Beeswax: Beeswax, while not taking advantage of generally in soaps, is an attractive additive to hand soaps because of the conditioning effect that it lugs the skin. It is sometimes contributed to soaps as a thickener, assisting in the mapping procedure.

Canola Oil: Canola oil is rich in crucial fats, and also in many cases, it is mixed with olive oil, making it a cheaper selection than pure olive oil. It's a high oleic oil, which suggests that it will take the longer trace. This is useful when you prefer to make specific soaps when processes, such as swirling, demands that you have a longer time to manage the particular soap.

Castor Oil: This oil is one more of the primary lather producing oil when used in a proportion of 5 to 10 percent. It acts as a humectant when mixed with various other oils and additionally is a superb choice for extremely fatted soaps.

Chocolate Butter: Will include a setup component to your soap meals. In the last thing, chocolate butter gives an obstacle on the skin that helps to safeguard along with keep dampness. Some individuals find the aroma of cocoa butter overpowering or disappointing. Unscented chocolate butter is readily available for soap making features:

Coconut Oil: One of the most effective oils to use to generate long-term soap. It is top-class in lathering and cleaning up effectiveness. The only shortcoming of coconut oil is that when used at a high portion, it can be possibly drying to some individual's skin.

Hazelnut Oil: With similarity to sweet almond oil in a commercial or residential building, this oil is light and easily absorbed right into your skin. Usually made use of in massage oils, it quickly takes in oil to include to your soaps and can alter olive oil in many solutions if the properties of the olive oil generate changes.

Hemp Oil: This is one of the most healing oils that you can add to your soap. Hemp or hemp seed oil is a superior option for cleansers that are crafted for dried skin, maturing skin, or hurt skin that needs more treatment.

Jojoba Oil: This is a light oil that is a remarkable conditioner. It can be a little bit more expensive than other oils; nonetheless, making use of jojoba in supper fatting or as a complimentary oil will enhance the oil in getting its numerous benefits.

Lard: This is among the least costly resources that you can use to produce top-notch soaps. Fat provides a superb, productive later on, and adds setting structures likewise. If any other scenting agents get made use of in the solvent, the scent is smooth and undetected in the finished work.

Olive Oil: This is among the most well recognize oils for soap making. Pure olive oil soap is creamy and classy. The majority of the minute, nonetheless, olive oil is used in mix with different other fuels to produce plentiful, moisturizing soaps. You can acquire olive oil as a food-grade oil or as a healing top quality oil. You will observe modest differences in the shade and scent of the olive oil, depending on which you choose. Bear in mind that lots of food-grade olive oils are cut with various other oils, so if you get straight off of your grocer's racks, ensure that the product you are obtaining has one hundred percent purity and from a credible supplier. It is alright to use olive oil that has an added oil included to it, merely have it in mind that the saponification worths of both (and even much more) oils might be various and adjustments might call for to be made in the amount of lye usually made use of for olive oil. You can also acquire recovery grade olive oil and additionally olive oil straight from craft and soap suppliers.

Hand Oil: Another easily used vegetable, palm, or oil is discovered in the majority of cooking area cupboards. Once again, if you purchase this oil straight from your food shop, ensure that you identify what the parts of the oil are. Palm oil is light in color along with scent and makes an excellent, neutral option for a lubricant.

Shea Butter: This thick, abundant butter is understood for retaining wetness and likewise can be taken advantage of instead of cocoa butter, which has a considerable extra fragrance that some individuals consider as unwanted. Shea butter is exceptional to use in face and hair care bars.

Pleasant Almond Oil: This oil is plentiful in vitamins along with minerals. It is furthermore really light in scent that makes it an exceptional addition to soaps that are established to be moisturizing and odorless. It is plentiful in healthy and balanced protein and absorbs swiftly best into the skin.

Tallow: There appear to be two separate institutions of concept concerning soaps that make use of pet fats. People either like them or do not like the tip of family pet items in their soaps and steer clear of. Beef tallow makes a harsh but incredibly light and moisturizing soap. Wax is most conveniently available from a lot of meat counters or butcher stores, but will need to be made before use, but can be purchased in a currently offered type from some distributors. An essential indicate remember is that if you are a little worried concerning using animal fats in your soap, thereby making use of wax in your soaps, you are assisting in making use of most components of an animal, including the fats which would only end up in a rubbish dump if an additional usage is not discovered for them. Instead of the typical assumption, making use of animal fats can indeed be ecologically positive.

Veggie Shortening: This is an outstanding alternative to hand oil and also as a replacement for pet fats. Vegetable shortening has a setup component to it and also creates a soap that is moderate and conditioning. Veggie minimizing is conveniently used from your supermarket, merely ensure that what you buy is pure veggie oil with no additional active ingredients.

Wheat Germ Oil: This is a type of oil that is abundant in vitamins, especially vitamins A, D, and E. The oil is exceptionally beneficial to the skin. It is a little thicker than the lighter oils of this listing and has a somewhat nutty and moderate fragrance to it, thereby making an attractive enhancement to sophistication bars.

Lye

Lye, which is referred to as sodium hydroxide or NaOH, is crucial for making soaps from square one at home. It is the treatment, called saponification, in between lye and the oils you pick that creates the soap. Soap manufacturers have been using lye for centuries, yet it is among the leading reasons that many individuals hesitate to try making their very own soaps in the house. The reason for this is that lye has somewhat a reputation. It is very caustic and can create severe chemical burns to the skin and can be deadly if eaten. Despite having this, with the right preventative procedures, there is no factor in being frightened of lye.

Apart from protection in usage, the next fear that several beginning soap makers have about lye is why you would certainly wish to use such a severe chemical in a substance that is established to be used on your skin? The reality is that when done correctly, the lye completely reacts with the oils to form a brand-new chemical material, referred to as soap. So, in a finished, cured product, lye doesn't proceed to irritate the skin.

Lye is readily available in many equipment stores, and you can make use of the knowledge in this publication to purchase your lye from a soap making representative or an added store that focuses on lye for craft purposes. This is so for two crucial reasons. The first of such rights is that the lye that you find in your neighborhood store is not in any way packaged with the soap maker in mind—the objective of that lye is basically to clean blocked pipelines or targets of similar nature. Sometimes, there are extra chemicals included in the lye, which would most certainly upload a security and security risk and be devastating to your soap. Second of all, the lye that you locate in a tools shop is generally in powder form since that is what jobs best for those planned usages.

The lye that you will acquire from a soap or craft carrier most typically is available in flake or pellet type. The distinction between pellets and powder makes no difference in your final product, but it can make a difference in the safety and security of the procedure.

Powdered lye is most likely to increase via the air, like powder often does, and develop a lye cloud that can worsen your skin, eyes, and sinus passages. Pellet lye can be quickly gauged along with put without that danger. What you choose to use is inevitably about you, but please maintain those safety and protection actions in mind when purchasing lye from hardware or residence taking care of the store.

Fragrances and colorants.

Whether or not you choose to make use of colorants and additional scents in your soap will depend significantly upon the designated function of the soaps you are making. You may be a great deal a lot more likely to add aromas and shades to your soaps if you are making soap that is suggested to be decorative or for specific craft objectives.

These two specified things can additionally establish your soap apart in addition to making soap, making a little more enjoyable for some individuals. That mentioned, it is vital to claim that several of the absolute best soaps that you can make are free along with natural of included colorants and fragrances letting the natural color and aroma of the oil come through.

However, what will be specified here is a bit of recommendation concerning both;

Fragrances: Who doesn't delight in a perfectly aromatic soap, with an aroma that works gently on the skin? The majority of times, when we choose up a brand-new bar of soap, the very first point a variety of us do is bring it to our nose to scent it. The fragrance usually happening from the components made use of in your soap, there are two means that you can deal with scenting your soap material; synthetically or generally.

Synthetic blends are scent oils in an alcohol base and can be bought from any soap or aesthetic supplier. While artificial aromas do not make use of a great deal of therapeutic worth, they provide massive options in sensory experiences. You can either acquire or mix virtually any fragrance you can visualize.

The disadvantage of the artificial mixture is that preliminary of all, and they can be annoying to the skin, which is not beneficial if you are seeking to create a healing bar of soap. Secondly of all, it takes a good deal of fragrance to scent a set of soap, which can be rather expensive. As an example, to scent the sort of solvents defined in this book, you would have to consist of 2 to 3 ounces of scent oil to develop a delicately fragrant soap. The 2nd difference suggested for scenting your soaps is to do it usually with natural fillers or crucial oils. Pads are active ingredients such as dried out blossom coffee properties, citrus passion, oatmeal, and dried out all-natural herbs. Including these components to your soaps will offer some restorative worth, fascinating structure, and a light fragrance to your softener.

Essential oils are the significances of plants and additionally blossoms that continue to be after a removal treatment. They are pure and potent. Numerous vital oils are used medicinally and therapeutically and can provide those identical residential properties to your soaps. Take note and have in mind that some essential oils can be bothersome to the skin, explicitly relaxing spicy oils such as cinnamon and ginger. The scent that originates from crucial oils is pure and a lot more potent than that from scent oils, so you do not require rather as much to smell a collection of soap. Essential oils can be costly or relatively cost-effective, relying on which you select. It takes around one to 2 ounces of required oils to scent a soap recipe the dimension of the ones consisted of in this publication.

Regardless of the form that you choose to make use of, the fragrance must be added at trace right before your soap goes directly into the mold and mildew and mildews.

Colorants: Just like with scent, you can choose to tint your soap typically through the enhancement of deliberate ingredients or unnaturally with using dyes explicitly created to add shade to soap. There is some discussion about which dyes or colorants are safe to make use of in your soaps. As a general regulation, you plan to stick with colorants that are as all-natural as viable, such as veggie dyes or oxides. Veggie dyes give you a lot more range of shades in addition to choices with tones. Oxides add much more natural-looking colors, mostly in shades of brownish, red, yellow, and pink. Soap will have a natural to it that is created by the oils that you select to usee. A couple of soap solutions will result in a pure white soap. If you choose to add colors to your soap, you will initially wish to include titanium dioxide, which can make your soap pure white, and then include your coloring, or the natural color of the soap might influence the result of your tinting components. When it involves adding suitable colorings to your soap; that, it is essential to remember that you need to buy your dyes from a trusted soap making vendor. Using coloring that is created for candlelight making or any various other objectives will not just affect the top quality of your soap, can be too toxic when made use of in a thing suggested being used topically.

You can tint your soap with gentler components that could similarly supply recovery worth to your formula. Instances of natural additives that will offer your soap color are flavors such as paprika, cinnamon, curry, and likewise turmeric. Othecolorants contain coffee, molasses, clay, vitamin E oil, carefully ground dried her, and algae just for circumstances. Much like with fragrance, many active ingredients used for making your soap must be included before placing right into the molds.

CHAPTER THREE

Forms of Soap Making

There are four various methods that you go about producing your soaps. Two of these techniques involve starting from scratch and promoting the chain reaction that transforms other materials right into a new soap. The two different methods include taking existing softeners and recreating them into something new. As you start soap making, you may want to try out each style to figure out which one you take pleasure the most. The four significant soap making types are:

Cold Processed: This is undoubtedly the most traditional approach to making soap. The process involves incorporating fats or oils with lye and also water. The resulting reaction produces a thick, soupy mixture referred to as soap that can then be poured into different kinds of mold and mildews where it will undoubtedly proceed to get harden until the pH level of the solvent is near neutral, and also the bar is sufficiently solid to be able to take on direct exposure to water without quickly liquefying. The reason for describing this sort of soap making as cold processed is that the only form of heat used is for melting the oils. The real heat involved does not come from the heat that you apply, but the heat that is produced in the chemical reaction between the lye, oils, and water.

Most bar soaps that you make use of our cold processed. This strategy enables you to develop your formulas, craft your bars to your demands. With a couple of safety and security precautions, this sort of soap making is a very satisfying craft. The only adverse effect of this procedure is that it is very time consuming, most notably when you consider the aging or curing duration, that the soaps go through before they are ready to be used. The curing period can take anywhere from many days to several months for a fully cured, pure olive oil soap.

Hot Processed: This is most likely the least previously owned method of soap making. Thermal processing is mostly used to create liquid soaps as well as is a little bit more of an involved process, so most homemade soap makers select not to get highly engaged with it. Hot processing soap includes using potassium hydroxide instead of sodium hydroxide (lye), and also the enhancement of heat to encourage the chain reaction that produces the soap. While cold processed soaps can be made in merely a couple of steps, a hot processed soap usually takes about twice as much action. A safety measure involved in warm processed soap is that the procedure reduces the soap pH level so much that you also need to add a preservative or the cleanser will face the risk of promoting fungi and mold. Due to the extremely detailed steps and the infrequency of use in modern times, we won't discuss the hot processed soap any further in this publication.

Hand Milled: This is an unbelievably simple way of making soaps that you do not need any calculations or formula to do. Hand milling or rebatching has to do with taking soaps that have previously been crafted either commercially or at home and making them right into new soaps. This is accomplished by shredding the existing soaps right into a dual central heating boiler or slow stove as well as melting them down to make a new soap.

You might be asking or wondering why you may have to do this. One important reason is that you can take scraps of old soaps and also create them right into functional bars. You may also make plain soaps and mix with scents or colorants and remold them right into brand-new forms.

What many soap manufacturers do is use rebatching as a means to conserve a batch of soaps that didn't quite fulfill their standards. Sometimes the structure is off, or soap might appear out of a mold and looking less than desired. At some other times, you may want to add a lot more emollient oil to an end product without bothering about the fuel being used up in the saponification process, or you recognize that your soap is a little hefty in the lye component and you wish to even it out without starting new.

Perhaps you made soap, and it turned out good, but upon reflection on what you did, you wish you had included some ground herbs or a light scent. Hand milling gives you the chance to do that.

Pour and also melt: This kind of soap making is by far the easiest and least time-consuming alternative. It does not include making any kind of soap. What you need to do instead is purchase blocks or pellets of pure glycerin soap and melt it to pour into your chosen molds. The Glycerin can be colored or perfumed as you wish. This kind of soap making is preferred for gift and also novelty soaps. The transparent nature of glycerin soap makes it suitable to display unique additives such as ornamental flowers and natural herbs, or even various other things such as seashells, jewels, and different other purely aesthetic fillers. This kind of soap is prominent for making kid's soap, which contains tiny little toys or ornaments as a sort of "reward." This kind of soap making calls for only the glycerin, a gadget to melt the soap in and your mold and mildews, along with essential security devices, naturally.

No matter what type of soap making you favor, keep in mind that the essence is to enjoy yourself. Experiment a little with the different sorts of soap making and choose which design you like considering the moment as well as the initiative involved with each, in addition to the creative flexibility each design brings you.

Each type of soap-making can be an art or a craft once you begin to add personal design or style right into it.

CHAPTER FOUR

Safety Precautions in Organic Soap Making

You might have heard that soap making can be harmful, and possibly at the hands of a negligent individual, that might be, but truthfully, that holds for almost about anything. The art of soap-making does not need to be a scary or intimidating process. All you need is an excellent understanding of the materials you are utilizing and a couple of safety precautions. As you start making soaps, you will develop your regimen that fits your style, and quickly you will be crafting soaps like a pro.

As you are starting, and as you continue to grow and establish your brand-new skill, you must always keep the following pieces of security suggestions in mind.

Take care of yourself. This suggests making sure that you are using all of the required protective gear consisting of shoes capable of protecting your feet from spills, long pants to cover your legs, long heat-resistant gloves, an apron to safeguard your clothes, safety glasses, and a hat or hair tie to keep your hair out of your face. It is likewise an excellent idea to stay preventive emergency treatment items convenient in case of an accident. These could consist of bandages, burn cream, and vinegar to reduce the effects of any part of the skin that lye touches.

Ensure you have all the required equipment ready to go. Also, be sure that you have read your developed recipe and know exactly what you need, and have premeasured as much as possible. You are having everything established will make the process much easier for you and will eliminate potential errors along the way.

Do not be scared of lye; however, do treat it with respect and care. Lye is dangerous and possibly fatal if consumed. The fumes may also be irritating to the skin, eyes, and lungs. Regularly utilize lye properly, keep it away from your face, work in a well-aerated area, and keep the toxin control number nearby, just in case.

Lye is reactive with aluminum, copper, and tin, so it is imperative to make sure that none of your tools that will enter into contact with the lye are made from these products. When possible, pick the pellet variety of lye, which is mostly easy to use in comparison with the powdered form, which can produce a lye cloud if you are not careful. Select heat-resistant glass, stainless steel, silicone, and wooden pieces of equipment. When water and lye meet, there is a chemical response that takes place.

It is a much safer process when lye is added to water than it is when you add the water to lye. Keep in mind that lye reactions produce heat and be prepared to manage your utensils.

If you were cooking, in the same way that you would.

How you label and store counts too. Keep security in mind even when you are not making soap. Label all of your soap making devices with a tag that designates it for soap making functions only. This will prevent you or somebody else present in your household from using the soap making equipment for other non-related purposes. Soap, as well as chemical residue, may remain on your computer, even after it is cleaned off, and other substances can interfere and dramatically affect the result of your soap making. Correct labeling will help to prevent this from happening. Store all of your equipment and products appropriately. Lye is a toxin and should be stayed out of reach of children, family pets, and anyone who is not acquainted with how to handle it.

Some of the fats and oils that you use in your soaps will have familiar names; however, if you purchase them from a soap making supplier or craft shop, they may not be the food-grade quality that is utilized in cooking. It is best not to run the risk of misinterpreting soap making oils for standard cooking oils. Have a designated cabinet or closet that can be locked for your soap making supplies if possible.

Products

Have it in mind, even when you end up being comfortable. After your number of batches of soap making, you will understand how straightforward it is to do. As you become more comfortable, it can be easy to adopt some standard security techniques. For instance, making soap can be a household activity; however, extreme caution should be used when children are included. Make sure that kids are properly secured, and keep the soap making for just older kids. If allowed in the soap making process, children who are impulsive and unpredictable present a severe risk to themselves and every other person in the location. Always keep your site well ventilated. Never leave your soap unattended throughout the procedure and operate in an area, and at a time when you understand, you will be free of diversions. A little prevention in these areas will go a lengthy method in keeping your soap, making it safe and satisfying.

SAFETY TIPS

• Always store lye in suitable air-tight containers. Label the boxes appropriately. A label with "DANGER! And an image with a skull and crossbones or a big red X in a circle may be used.

• Keep containers out of reach of family pets and children.

• When dealing with lye, you'll need to wear a long-sleeved shirt, safety goggles, rubber gloves, long trousers, socks and shoes.

• It's an excellent concept to put on a disposable face mask while handling or working with lye.

• At the point of mixing your lye-water solution, don't forget always to get the lye added to the water, and never do it the other way around. If you choose to add the water to the lye, the chemical reaction might cause some of the mixture to spill on you!

• Add the lye gradually while stirring the liquid carefully. It will get quite hot, so make sure to always begin with freshwater, never warm or hot water.

• Prepare the lye and water service in a well-ventilated location. Make sure that the stove range is on and that if you use the kitchen sink, the window above the sink is open. Ensure you choose to mix it outside if it isn't windy, and the air temperature is comfortable.

• If you find some of the lye solution on your skin, rinse thoroughly with lukewarm water, then spray some vinegar on your skin. Keep a spray bottle handy for such emergencies.

CHAPTER FIVE

Methods of Soap Making

Where do you start, and what precisely are the steps to making the best homemade soap? Well, that depends upon what sort of soap you are making. In this chapter, we will go through the steps involved in the conventional soap making methods:

THE REBATCHING METHOD

The rebatching method is a fast and straightforward technique. As the name of the technique suggests, it is often used to rebatch if there were any errors or if you did not like the form of the mold and mildew or messed it up throughout the design process. This method can also be used if you wish to get a feel of the soap-making Do It Yourself experience without getting additional tools. Readymade soap never thaws quickly, that is why, although you will warm it as we described in the thaw and pour method, you will add few tablespoons of water, glycerin, etc. to soften up the mix, then with heat-resistant handwear covers, you will include your soap thaw in a Ziploc bag and massaged it so make it into a mushy structure.

Comparable to the melt and pour process, you can include the color and fragrance to your mix in the rebatching approach and then allow it solidify. This will take 5-7 days, but as you wait for all the water to evaporate. Rebatched soap doesn't have the most aesthetic appearance or feel, but it is a suitable solution to ruined soap or if you desire to add your very own color and fragrance to existing soap.

This method bypasses the disadvantage of adding things that get damaged by lye, such as lavender buds, which turn brown with the application of lye. You may also use colors that are sensitive to the pH of lye that you can not apply in the cold process. When used in the cooling process, similar is the instance with being able to make use of light fragrances with the rebatching method, which obtains concealed.

The benefits of both rebatching and thaw and put methods is that you do not need to handle lye, which is afraid by numerous people as it is a solid alkali. Additionally, you do not even require a whole lot of components, to begin with, or intricate computations, and you can immediately start to enjoy the soap once it solidifies. On the other hand, you have very little control over the raw ingredients being used as you are starting with something that someone else made, you don't control everything from scrape as with the cold method. The freezing process is likely to be the best process for you if you desire to be the master of the experiment and absolutely in control of what goes in your soap.

MELT AND POUR METHOD

This is among the most straightforward soap making processes and saves a great deal of time. In this procedure, you can use a premade soap base that has gone through the saponification process instead of hanging out blending fats with an alkali such as lye, which can be time-consuming as it needs even more preparation time. A readymade soap base includes glycerin and fatty acids along with various other all-natural ingredients.

The thaw and put approach is the ideal option if you are a newbie, still checking out the arena and wishes to play it secure. All you have to do is buy a premade solid soap base rather than making it from scrape, and you are prepared to make use of the soap once it solidifies, no unneeded awaiting a remedy time to pass, such as with chilly procedure.

How this method functions:

Head to a neighboring arts and crafts store and try to find a premade soap base—one of the very best options to purchase is white premade soap bases or the clear glycerin. Do not use a bar of soap for this as it is not the very same point and will give you a problem while melting.

The next action would be to thaw your strong premade soap base. To quicken this process, use a sharp knife to cut bench right into little 1-inch portions. Do not stress over exact dimensions right here. The objective is to have smaller items as opposed to one big piece as smaller pieces will certainly melt quicker.

Add your cut chunks in a microwave and heat for about 30 seconds. Take out the meal and stir your melted contents after that reheat once again for one more 30 seconds after that get to stir once again. Next step, repeat this cycle heating 30 seconds, then stir until you eventually feel that the consistency of your melted soap as completely liquidity with no lumps or hard chunks in between. When your whole soap base has melted, that is. Do not overheat it past that point.

Some people don't own a microwave in their residence. It is feasible to change it with a pan full of water to develop a water bathroom. Heat the water and then place a glass recipe and let it float in the warm water. Place your soap base portions in the glass recipe and watch it thaw with the warm that moves from the warm water to the glass bowl and, consequently, to the soap base portions that thaw eloquently. Do not neglect to stir. When your soap base, eliminate the recipe from the sauce frying pan, has entirely melted and doesn't have any swellings.

Allow your soap thaw to cool off to around 50 level Celsius. Do not add your crucial oils or color while the thaw is still hot. Don't allow it cool down to the point of hardening. Include 2-3 drops of your wanted dye depending on the color intensity you desire. If you are using a powdered color, liquify 2-3 tablespoon of your powdered dye in some liquid glycerin as you can't include the power straight to your thaw; otherwise, the color will not obtain dispersed evenly. It is always terrific to add a pleasant fragrance to your soap. For a quantity of soap measuring 1 pound, you can add 1 tablespoon of scent oil or half a tablespoon of essential oil. Make sure you use the ones labeled for soap making and not candle oils, to ensure they are soft and friendly on your skin.

Stir all your included color and fragrance drops before the last step. The final action would be to pour your colored and fragranced merge into a mold of your choice after that let it cool generally for 12-24 hours. When your soap has wholly strengthened, take it out of the image and mildew, and it would await usage promptly. Make sure the sides have dried completely.

THE HOT PROCESS

This procedure is like the cold process but entails using heat pots and "food preparation"the soap instead of doing it cool.

THE COLD PROCESS.

In soap making, the chilly process is the dragon level of all levels. The gameplay becomes a little bit more complicated, but don't fret we have obtained your back, and we are here to direct you through it detailed. The incentive right here is that there are limitless opportunities to exactly how you can make your end product in terms of colors, forms, and all-natural additions. Furthermore, you can 100% guarantee that your soap is homemade from square one.

Let us begin with the necessary active ingredients you will need for making soap using the cold process:

- Lye flakes and clean distilled water.
- A resource of fat, whether pet fat or veggie oil.
- A natural soap dye of your option, whether liquid or powder (preferred but optional).
- Soap pot together with various other equipment, which we will certainly go over in even more information shortly.
- An essential oil or fragrance of your option (favored but optional) A mold of your wanted shape.
- A tidy environment to work in and a cool, dry location to allow the soap treatment in.

- For looks, flowers, or scrubs (optional).
- A convenient recipe to follow

How It Works

The essence of the cold soap making procedure is preparing lye and a source of fat and blending it.

1-Making the Lye remedy.

The first action is to prepare the lye service. For specific quantities, you will need to describe your picked recipe.

Using your kitchen area scale or digital scale, put the glass bottle, and set the size to no. Following, you would be adding distilled water, as indicated in your recipe. Some recipes suggest weight; consequently, you will undoubtedly position the pitcher on the range.

Various other recipes suggest volume; therefore, you can use your determining cup.

Next, it is time to gauge up the lye solution. Do so with the use of your mason jar with a tight, protected cover. Lye is an antacid and can hurt your skin. That is the reason you need to handle it using gloves and while using your safety and safety goggles. If any type of lye flakes stick to your glove, remove them instantly. Place the Mason jar and its cover on the scale and set it to zero. Include the lye flakes up until the range suggests the weight suggested in your picked recipe. You can change the Mason container with a plastic bottle. Do not use this bottle for anything else other than handling lye during your soap making process.

After your weights are established based on suggested in your recipe, time to blend them up, be careful about this action. Ensure you add the lye to the water bit by bit and not put the water to the lye. Gently start including your lye flakes to the pitcher having water. Add it little by little from a safe but close range to prevent dashes. To liquify the lye suitably, stir the blend carefully and gradually, once more without spraying. As both react, you will start to listen to fizzy sounds or feel the heat, which is normal. Do not let the solution touch your skin directly. Keep your goggles and handwear covers on. After mixing, wash the item you used to mix with immediately. Do not neglect to cover your bottle, including your freshly combined lye water, and let it go for a long time. See to it is connected firmly and put in a safe place away from animals or children. Caution needs to remain in mind around lye or lye water always.

2-Preparing the oils.

Get your useful scale once more because we will evaluate out your picked oil as per the recipe, using the same technique of including the soap pot or a glass pitcher on the scale and establishing it to zero. It is better to use the soap pot to weigh stable oil, such as chocolate butter, while handling the glass bottle for liquid fuel such as olive oil. Slowly add the oil to your container until the range hits the preferred weight.

Examples of substantial fat resources include; Cocoa butter, coconut, or palm.

Examples of fat liquid resources include; Castor oil, canola oil, olive oil, sunflower oil.

Melt it initially using a sauce frying pan if you are using a stable oil. This will undoubtedly shorten the action for you as you need to heat your chosen oil anyway. The oil needs to warmth slowly, so use tool warmth and stir delicately. You require to enjoy the temperature level of your oil using the thermostat and transform off the warm when it reaches about 110 F. However, you can not add it right now to the lye water combination.

The oils temperature level requires to go down to 100 F before it can be mixed with the lye water. If you are making use of stable oil, all the stable oil has pertained to a melt. Include the liquid fuels after all the stable fats melt if your recipe indicates a blend of solid and liquid oils. Nevertheless, monitor your temperature level once more, as this will decrease the temperature of the total oil mixture. Keep in mind, and you need it to be about 100 F when you mix it thoroughly with the use of lye water.

3- Add the Lye water to the Oil base.

Once you blend these 2, the saponification reaction will be instant, and the mixture will turn gloomy, suggesting a chemical response where the lye and oil react in the existence of warmth to make soap.

The lye is no more chemically lye; that is why hand-crafted soap is risk-free on the skin. It no more has lye as it all changed to soap when it combined with the warm oil. Since from right here on the process will happen swiftly, you need to have your preferred additions on standby, for instance, your fragrance containers, crucial oils, dye, spatulas, and so on. Carefully add the lye blend to the warm oil in the soap pot. You will see a color modification in which the mixture will certainly start to be cloudy. Mix delicately, ideally with a stick blender, although keep it shut off now. After you have poured in all your lye water combination, maintain the glass bottle that had it in a safe area for the time being till you safely cleanse it later. Right currently, you need to stay with your brand-new combination.

If you are using a stick blender, transform it on now and allow it to mix the combination in short intervals of a couple of seconds and repeat until you feel that both your lye water and oil have entirely mixed till you reach trace. Trace is gotten to when the combination has emulsified, significance, when the mix is left later, it will maintain getting thicker and thicker with time as a component of the process.

How to Recognise When You Have Reached Trace Point

The stick blender or food processor has severely sped up the procedure of saponification, and getting to trace takes seconds compared to hrs making use of regular mixing. If your mixture still has glowed oily liquidly floating in between strokes, then all the oil has not combined totally with your lye water. You will reach trace when the velvety uniformity begins to thicken somewhat and has a uniform consistency instead of having both oily and thick uniformities.

The Importance of Reaching Trace Point?

For many factors, chief amongst them is that since the mapping point is the factor where all the mixture has emulsified and came to be soap particles rather than oil and lye, that means putting the mixture before achieving trace leads to having incomplete soap. This will result in flawed soap or incompletely developed soap. You will still have lye bits in your soap, which will be hazardous to your skin. Consequently, you require to maintain stirring till you think cake-like batter consistency without glistening oil streaks. This mixture will certainly also be easy to pour into a mold and will undoubtedly be of uniform consistency; you will not locate oil leaking from the batter

It is safe to include your color and scent in the light trace action before the thick medium trace step begins. Medium trace has a thicker consistency than a light hint, resembling that of a pudding uniformity. You can evaluate for it by trickling some of the batters from the blender or food processor, and it will form visible soap touches on the mixture's surface; the method delicious chocolate touches on a cake. This is one of the most convenient to add your all-natural robust additives such as leaves, exfoliate, petals, etc

The final trace uniformity is that which resembles a thick dessert batter. That is the trace uniformity that will adapt to its shape when put right into a mold, which is what you want. To reach this trace phase, you require to maintain stirring with the stick blender or food processor. If you desire to create soap frosting, you will need to immensely enlarge your trace to obtain soap uniformity for icing or ornamental purposes.

Remember a very vital inaccurate trace indication when you use an active trace if it has not been completely thawed and home heating, it can quickly cool during the mixing procedure and give the incorrect feeling of solidifying mixture. At the same time, it is not hardening because of saponification, but it is because of the tightening of the stable fat. Because of that, ensure that it sufficiently.

Aspects That Can Affect Trace Consistency

No doubt, using a stick will make you get to a tool, and thick consistency trace much faster than stirring by hand. Consider mixing by hand using a spatula when you reach thin trace consistency if you would, such as to give your color and scent some time to mix well.

Some additives and fragrances such as clay accelerate the trace procedure and make your combination thicken quickly. Be conscious about such enhancements and the timing and technique of stirring. It is better to switch over to hand-operated mixing after including fragrance.

4- Adding your individual touch.

After reaching the desired state, and before it is also thick, you can currently include your selected fragrance, essential oils, and additives such as natural herbs, petals, or natural exfoliants. Carefully mix and make sure your enhancements are thoroughly incorporated within the batter. We will talk about some instances of exfoliants and vital oils.

Coloring your Soap.

Among the gorgeous elements of making your very own soap is that you can select the color of your soap. You can have your color as one solid color for the entire bar, or you can obtain creative with color touches. If you intend to have a dull-colored bar of soap, add your preferred color dye. Ensure it is soap dye and not candlelight color. You can add more coloring to boost the color intensity of the soap, but don't overdo it. Mix well to disperse the color equally.

If you intend to attempt innovative methods such as the touch method, get about half a cup or a mug of your soap individually in your measuring mug and add the color to it and mix thoroughly. Put the remainder of your soap batter in your preferred mold and mildew and carefully pour your colored mix to the image.

While using a rubber or wooden spatula, start pulling colored streaks from the shaded corner to design the soap batter that is depending on the mold far from the edge. You can swirl around the color to develop your preferred pattered, but don't overdo it to ensure that you do not blend the color with the entire mix. The charm of this step is that you can get imaginative with color designs and patterns or even color combinations of your choice.

Put your Mixture into a mold and mildew.

Now, your blend is prepared to be poured into your preferred mold and mildew. As you would uniformly put a cake mix into a mold and mildew, do so with your soap batter. A handy rubber spatula will help you to scrape off the remainder of the soap batter in your soap pot and right into the mold and mildew. Ultimately, drink the mold and mildew carefully to equally disperse the soap batter in your image to get a consistent bar. To obtain a soap bar with a flat surface area, you require to travel the surface of the mix and also it out with the back of a spoon or with a rubber spatula.

In some cases, air bubbles would collect in your blend throughout the putting step. You will certainly need to eliminate those. Delicately tap your mold and mildew against the kitchen top to release any bubbles. Finally, leave your soap to heal in a cozy and a refuge.

Now it is the right time to leave your mold and mildew to harden for about 24 hrs. Then, prepare to take it out of the frame and cut it into acceptable dimensions. It is best to let those bars cure for four weeks before using it, although it is risk-free to use right now. Don't neglect to clean all the devices you used exceptionally well with warm water and soap while still wearing your goggles and handwear covers.

DECORATING YOUR SOAP

You can get innovative with your soap, starting with picking the shape of the mold and mildew or producing your very own impression. Another fantastic method would be to swirl the soap or use specific divider panels in such a way that develops new designs. The malleability of soap enables you to make it into any shape you prefer conveniently. You can also reduce the soap into small heart-shaped items and put them in a jar with a cute note or shape it as cookies or anything you desire.

When developing, Coloring is another terrific thing to get creative with. You can build masterpieces and color mixes. It is a fantastic suggestion to have ideas on exactly how to make your soap.

You can likewise use the edge of the spoon to etch patterns in the soap, insert petals, diamonds, shine, natural herbs, the secret message inside — actually, anything you want. Particular flowers can include a glamorous touch to your soap. It is as much as your creative thinking. You can likewise purchase a stamp that makes cute forms externally of the solvent or engraves your trademark.

The product packaging of the soap itself is an essential consider how expert and attractive your soap looks. Ensure the soap edges are reduced nicely and smoothly and evenly. Invest in some creative and adorable packaging, make it personal, and make it lovely.

CHAPTER SIX

The need for Natural and Organic Soaps

With the availability of many varieties of soap in the market, you might question why some people choose to make organic natural soaps at home. The processes of making organic homemade soaps might appear like a great deal of difficulty considering that you can easily buy from a shop, and the waiting duration can seem barely worth it to those who have never made soap before.

People have different reasons for deciding to make homemade organic soaps, but there are many great reasons amongst them. If you are questioning the possibilityofmakingorganic handmade soaps, think about why you are doing so. While you're at it, think about these other general reasons for choosing to make organic homemade soaps:

It's a Good Way to Recycle

There are four techniques used when making soap, and among the methods, the melt and pour plan is a great way to recycle old solvents! If you are the type of individual who has felt continuously bad about getting rid of the little soap that gets left behind in soap containers, (you understand, the kind that is too little to use, but appear a waste to be discarded?), then this hobby can be your answer! The melt and put approach will let you melt these soaps down, blend it up again, and produce a new soap! You get to conserve cash and the earth!

It's Great for Skin Care

When you make homemade soaps at home, you care for your skin much better. Not because the procedure of making the soap assists your skin, but since the soaps themselves are so much better for your skin that business products.

These are simply 4 of the many terrific reasons that you should start to make homemade soaps. Nevertheless, be conscious of the fact that if you have never made soap previously, you might have to buy some brand-new equipment. This is another indicate think about before beginning the pastime.

It Can Turn into a Business

Many individuals who make homemade soaps quickly find that their hobby can be turned into a lucrative business. Lots of individuals have developed rewarding sideline services from their soap making hobby since it is one of the best ways to put all the excess or additional soap to good use!

It's a Great Hobby

Making soap is a great pastime to have! It's one of those pastimes that have a tangible impact. It usually makes the enthusiast feel terrific every time they see the fruit of their labor. When you make soap, you will get this feeling. It's the kind of hobby that you can do to de-stress yourself and indulge yourself at the same time. It will give you a chance to invest time with your kids while doing something efficient together if you desire to. It must assist keep your creativity inspired and flowing, which tends to flow over to other locations of your life!

CHAPTER SEVEN

What To Consider When Choosing Homemade Soap Recipe

If you are beginning in soap making, you must pick the ideal homemade soap recipe. Choosing a method that is too made complex will generally end in aggravation and squandered components. Below are some ideas you can use to discover a great soap recipe to begin within your soap making adventure.

1 - Choose the Right Method

While it might seem apparent, you need first to choose the soap making approach you desire to find out before you begin looking for a recipe. If you intend to discover how to make homemade soap entirely from scratch, you'll want to start with the cold procedure.

2 - Make Sure It's Simple

It would probably be finest not to try your hand at a complicated recipe right off the bat. Start with a simple method that uses a couple of fundamental active ingredients. Then you can move up to other techniques like swirling and embedding botanicals as soon as you can make this natural soap well and have mastered the basics.

3 - Use the Homemade Soap Recipe from a reputable Source

Due to the nature of soap making and the need for precise measurements, the recipe you choose must come from a recognized source. You might do whatever right, but the soap would not come out appropriately.

4 –Go for a Recipe with Ingredients You Like

You might be lured to make a soap that has an aroma that a member of the family or buddy likes; however, it is best to stay with what you like in the beginning. Because you will desire to make a batch or two before you are all set to let others attempt out your soap, this is. You do not wish to be stuck with a cleanser that has a scent that you do not delight in for that first couple of batches!

5 - Choose a Fun Recipe

While it may seem like the only fun recipes are the complex ones, there are plenty of simple recipes that are a blast to make! Browse, and you will be sure to run into sufficient methods to keep you busy.

CHAPTER EIGHT

Common Mistakes In Homemade Soap Making

Homemade soap making lets you enjoy the exciting process of fats and lye mixed with water to create moderate bar soap. It appears almost like magic. It is a simple process to perform, but it's easy to make mistakes. Here are a few of mine;

1. Insufficient scent.

Scent oils are pricey, and it's appealing to use just a little less. Recipes often don't require enough of the stinky oils, either. You either used oils that don't work in soap making, or you used too little fragrance if it does not smell.

2. Poor Recipe.

Some recipes are just flat incorrect probably because the author of the formula was ignorant about how to design soap.

3. Mistakes in measurement.

Little recipes are more challenging to solve than large ones. It is crucial to make use of the right quantities in the process of soap-making. That's why methods that use weights are better than recipes that use measures like cups etc.

4. Insufficient stirring.

Different soap-making recipes take different times to begin tracing or hardening as it's called. You can design methods that discover quickly, but in any case, you keep stirring up until the soap traces. It can take 10 minutes, or it can take hours.

5. Wrong tools.

Cutting soap is one process that can get you hurt. Attempt to get soap cutting tools, so you do not use knives to cut soap.

The art part takes practice. Making soap is a great pastime and can be a lucrative little organization.

CHAPTER NINE

Making Homemade Organic Soaps More Creative

Essential soap recipes can assist you in making homemade soap that is great to use, and enjoyable to produce. Nevertheless, there is more than merely an organic solvent on the marketplace these days. There are soaps with lovely things embedded in them, swirls, attractive colors, and exceptional scents.

There is no limit to the variety of options you can develop if you simply utilize a little creativity. If you would instead make something a little more intriguing than merely a first soap, here are a couple of options to think about.

Scents

After your soap has developed a trace, you can include various aromas. You do not have to stick with the flower scents you find in the majority of shop soap. Simply remember that you never need ever to add a smell before the solvent has developed a trace, given that the lye can degrade it.

Colors

Soap dyes and colors are an excellent way to include interest to a plain white bar of soap. There are both natural and artificial dyes offered on the marketplace. The benefits of synthetic dyes to make homemade soap include their brightness and longevity. The advantages of natural colors for making handmade soap include their propensity to be less annoying to delicate individuals, and their natural origin. Natural dyes are often less fantastic and lightfast than synthetics. Both are incorporated in the same way as fragrances - after the trace has appeared. Some stains might be impacted by uncured soap. Do not feel trapped into only making one color, either. Make two batches of soap and color them differently, then swirl them together in the mold for striking marbled soaps.

Additions

You can include things besides color and scent, too. For example, some people embed natural sponge into their soaps, developing a soap and sponge in one. Others add oatmeal and other compounds to soap bars to produce an abrasive exfoliant soap. You can make homemade soap with all kinds of things in it. Dried flowers can be beautiful in solvents, and beads of oil can provide extra moisture. There are all sorts of innovative and appealing additions that can become part of your organic soap, making it something special.

As you can see, a standard soap recipe can be extra special by adding merely a couple of touches. You can make homemade soap only the way you like it.

CHAPTER TEN

Curing and Cutting Cold Process Soap

As soon as you have made your cold process soap, you will be itching to use it! While this is entirely reasonable, you will obtain far better and more secure results by sufficing and leaving it to heal and harden for 4 to 6 weeks.

Unmoulding.

Once your soap has cooled, you can unpack the insulation and eliminate it from the mold. You can take it right out if you have made use of a silicone or a lined shell.

If it is showing some indications of sticking, pop it in the fridge freezer for a couple of hours and after that get rid of the soap. If you have put the detergent directly into a plastic mold, you will need to freeze it for approximately 8 hours before attempting to remove it. Place the soap properly on greaseproof (wax) paper, to defrost it properly, remember to use handwear covers when handling it.

After you have unmolded the soap, you can get ready to dry and cure completely. At this stage, it is essential to use suitable gloves to take care of the solvent, which may be caustic in places. You can use a big knife, a cheese cutter, or a soap-cutting device to reduce your soap into bars all set to dry. The quicker you cut the solvent, the better coating you will carry benches.

Soap is softer and also much easier to cut and adjust right after unmoulding, and this is a great time to cut out any type of shape from the soap using cookie cutters or customize it with the use of stamps. A bar of soap that has been kept or left uncut for weeks will have a hard outer edge that has dried, and this can collapse when cut.

Curing.

As soon as the soap has been reduced, you will require to leave it cozy and someplace completely dry for it to cure for the next four to six weeks. There are two factors for treating soap: first of all, the prolonged cure time will guarantee that all sodium hydroxide (caustic soft drink) is counteracted, and also secondly, the longer the soap treatments, the tighter the bar ends up being. While treating, the water will undoubtedly vaporize from the drying soap, and it will shrink by at the very least 10 percent, making it harder and much longer long-lasting.

The soap has to be outlined with voids in between benches to permit complete blood circulation of the air and transformed every few weeks to allow the side of the soap remaining on the rack to have access to the atmosphere. Damp, severe problems are not significant.

For soap bars, as they will not solidify and can often sweat and come to be slimy to touch. It is likewise not suggested to keep soap in plastic, as this avoids it from drying.

PH Testing.

It is essential to pH test your soap always to ensure that it is safe for usage. To do that, dissolve a shaving of soap right into a small amount of water and dip a pH strip right into the mix. The pH needs to be ten or lower and, in many cases, will undoubtedly be pH 8 or 9.

When the soap is higher than pH 10, leave it for a few weeks to treat after that evaluate it once more.

Gelling.

Typically talking, if your soap is made at the higher end of the temperature scale and insulated well, it will undoubtedly undergo a reaction called gelling. Gelling is where the soap warms up, liquefies and turns translucent from the center, working its method to the exterior. It will speed up the if this is permitted to take place saponification procedure and reduce the cure time. If your soap gels alls the way to when you unmould it, the edges should have a pH of below 10.

In some cases, the gel is insufficient, and also you can know this by the color difference between the edges and the center of the soap. The gelled part will be darker, and you will see a lighter colored ring around the edges. To be safe, it is most advisable to cure the soap for the recommended four to six weeks, as this is will certainly make sure that all soap is saponified and also is solid enough to be used. When you carry out pH examination for your soap, it might have a pH of above 10 (generally, the strip will undoubtedly be purple). Usually, if you re-test in a few weeks, the pH will have gone down to under ten as the saponification is completed.

Using Soap Recipes

Many individuals will certainly have acquired a hand-crafted bar of soap and wondered why it went soft and also did not last extremely long compared to commercial bars. Handmade soap needs air around it to enable it to dry out in between usages. An excellent soap recipe with a lot of deep slats can help in the production of a soap that will last a lot longer and maintain its firmness. Additionally, make an old fashioned soap on a rope (see Soap on a Rope), which keeps air circulating all around it between usages.

Embellishing and Packaging Soap.

There are many means to decorate, personalize, or package your soap for gifts, wedding favors, or to sell. If you are offering your soap for sale as a business venture, make inquiries on the legal requirements, as there are stringent legal demands to be met before you can sell your soap. You will find a lot of ideas online from sites such as Pinterest, where other soap makers post pictures of enhanced or packaged soaps. Be extremely mindful not to copy others, as designs might be copyrighted; instead, you may use these pictures to get suggestions and make your very own unique productions.

Embedding Botanicals.

Cloves or other embedded if you desire to decorate your soap with rosebuds products, such as shells or rocks, you ought to do so quickly after cutting. At the beginning of curing, the soap is still soft and also malleable, and as it dries out, the embedded items will be clung in the dry solvent.

Using Stamps

At this stage, you can additionally individualize your soap with a rubber or acrylic stamp. General stamps with concepts or mottos, such as 'Handmade,' can be purchased from soap supply companies. Alternatively, you can design your very own rubber or acrylic stamp with an individual message, logos or initials, and also have it produced online.

Rubber Stamps.

Rubber stamps give a mild, printed appearance to the soap and can only be used promptly after removing, while the soap is still soft. To use a rubber stamp, use it quickly after removing it. To make use of it appropriately, you should put it on the area you wish to mark and design it with a rubber club. This can take some practice, once that is achieved, it gives a lovely and professional look.

Acrylic Stamps.

Acrylic stamps are much more complicated, and the soap will undoubtedly need to have been entrusted to dry for at least two weeks before using them. Twoweekswillsufficeif, the stamp design is essential; however, the plan is more detailed; you may need to leave it a week or two longer. Merely line the stamp up where you prefer it and push it into the soap mold.

Packaging and Wrapping.

Once your soap has set and cured, you can start to consider product packaging and covering for gifts. Soap needs to be exposed to air, so it is not recommended to wrap it in plastic or cellophane as this will encourage the appearance of moisture around the soap. Giftwrap, greaseproof(wax) paper, and also fabric can be used to wholly or partly wrap the soap and still allow it to take a breath. When covering is with, I discover the simplest means to secure the solvent is a fantastic thaw glue gun, which will hold well and also completely dry quickly.

1. Greaseproof (wax) paper, pretty ribbon, and a transcribed message on a parcel tag: for a rustic, confident appearance.

2. Brownish paper and ribbon: a sophisticated and straightforward coating.

2. Brownish paper and ribbon: This helps to achieve a simple and attractive finish.

3. Scraps of vintage or flower textile: a merely trendy wrap.

4. Greaseproof raffia, bow, and paper: excellent for enhancing the color of the soap and also any type of stamp to be used with it.

5. Gold paper, green twine, and wax seals: This is one of the best cheery gift wrap individualized with your seal.

6. Smooth ribbon: allows the soap's fragrance to be released.

7. Rosebuds and also bow: push rosebuds right into the top of the soap while soft and also include an adorable complementary bow.

8. Present cover: ideal for keeping the scent and making it look better.

9. Mulberry paper, ribbon, and lavender sprig: extravagant documents available in several colors. Put a sprig of lavender, rosemary, or heather into the fabric for better favor.

10. Greaseproof, twine, and seal: a traditional finish soap. This type of stamp leaves a deeply embedded appearance and is deficient for branding.

Fixing

Typically both cold process and melt and pour soap production are straightforward, and if you comply with the directions, you will not have any type of troubles. Nonetheless, the most productive people have batches that fail, and here are a couple of instances of what can take place and exactly how to fix each problem;

Issue: Thesoap just partially gelling or not gelling in any way.

The majority of problems occur from heat loss and poor mixing; If you have to stir or whisk for a very long time, you will lose warmth from the set, and this might lead to the soap partially gelling or not gelling in any way. This may lead to acid soap for the first couple of weeks until it has had a chance to cure and completely saponify. If you discover that it is taking you more excellent than twenty minutes to get to trace, you may intend to attempt the stick blender or food processor strategy (see Advanced Strategies) to speed the procedure up and decrease heat loss.

White swirls through the soap

Now and then, you will discover white swirls running through areas of the soap, usually towards the surface. These swirls will certainly be caustic when pH evaluated, also when the remainder of the soap tests at pH 8-- 9. This would take place if the soap was not traced when poured into the mold (generally the soap from the bottom of the pan in the sides). To fix this, you need to make sure that the soap is well-stirred, particularly at the end of the pan.

Oil on the surface area of the soap

When a thin layer of oil appears on the side or surface of the soap, you can wipe it away and also cure the soap as typical, testing the pH. If there is only a slim layer, it should not influence the pH of the solvent, as the recipes contain a minimum of 6 percent excess oil. If the soap becomes separated and there is a considerable amount of fat, the soap should be discarded, as it will be caustic. You might find methods for rebatching soap online, but this is not generally suggested for caustic sets.

Pockets of caustic liquid with the soap

You might find on reducing what looks like a truly great set of soap that you have big or little pockets with fluid coming out of them. If this fluid is caustic, you have a problem, and the soap should be discarded. When the liquid is pH ten or lower, it is most likely to be oil or water, in which case you can grate the soap and reprise it into balls and also remake it into bars.

Soap crumbles and cracks despite having highpH.

Soap that has not gelled is often brittle and when compressed forms, what looks like a regular bar of soap. This is typically as a result of heat loss. To prevent this, try the stick mixer method (see Advanced Techniques) at the higher end of the temperature range.

Thin white powdery substance appears on the surface area.

If the soap examinations well, this is generally a cosmetic response and can be scuffed away and used as regular. To avoid this, cover the soap with a cling film (plastic wrap) or plastic before protecting it.

Soap stars to embed in the pan.

This takes place where the soap thickens very much before you have the chance to put it into the molds. Specifically, it usually occurs when essential oils or fragrances, such as clove, are made use of. You can press the soap into the particular molds, and it will be great once it has been cut, gelled and cured. It will look somewhat rustic and lumpy, but it will undoubtedly be entirely usable. To avoid this, you can replace fifty percent of the olive pomace in the recipe for additional virgin, which will reduce trace and permit you more time. Remember to add the scent at a light trace.

Advanced Techniques.

You can start to move when you have understood the fundamental strategies in this publication on advanced soap production. We will cover sophisticated techniques and recipes in this area.

Using a Stick Mixer

Among the most significant issues with soap production is warmth loss and insufficient stirring. If you take more than twenty mins to get your set to trace, you will shed a great deal of heat, which might lead to a variety of the problems described in the.

Troubleshooting

At this stage, and when you are confident that you have mastered the whisking technique, you can switch over to using a stick blender or food processor. Stick blenders are generally made use of in bigger sets where a whisk is not an alternative; however, if you are making use of a small pan on these recipes, the deepness ought to be enough to use a blender or food processor.

Stick mixers will reduce the tracing time to a couple of mins, but with that said comes the distinct opportunity of overtrading your set and having areas that are not traced. The very best method is to use brief bursts of about five secs, followed by stirring well with the blender turned off. This will guarantee you obtain trace throughout, without going too much.

Essential Oils.

It is recommended to choose when you are trying out with essential oil blending two or three types of oil that you position a decrease on a paper. If you desire more of a specific oil, and until you have a blend that you delight in. Note the proportion of fats, and you can deduce from that for your set.

As a basic guideline for home soap making, I suggest an optimum of three percent basics or fragrance using the base oils and also sodium hydroxide (caustic) as the quantity to work out your percent. For instance, if you have 1.2 kg (12lb 10 1/2 oz) of base oils and 170g (6oz) of salt hydroxide, you would certainly use 41g (1 1/2 oz) of a solitary essential oil or a mix of several oils to that weight.

Superfatting

The bulk of cold procedure recipes in this publication have excess fat in the base recipe at six percent. You can go as much as eight percent excess fat in your base recipe-- this is called superfatting your soap, and it makes the soap more hydrating— anything beyond moisturizing. Anything past eight percent makes the bench also soft and is not suggested.

You can additionally-super fat as much as 8 percent after trace making use of valuable beneficial oils as a supplement; this has been done in the soft soap, where we have added an added 15g (1/2 oz) of calendula oil as a supplement, making the recipe 8 percent excess fat in overall.

SECTION TWO

SOAP MAKING RECIPES

A standard soap recipe for starters must not consist of many fragrance, ingredients, essential oils, or color. For your initial set of production, stick with one that runs not more than three to four oils, lye, and water. The recipes in this part of the book are ideal for first-timers. As soon as you have made some sets of soaps and made sure that you'll seek more sophisticated recipes, you should start working with a lot more challenging methods!

Please keep in mind that all the recipes in this publication mainly make use of grams and set up for determining in the most standard device of ounces.

Cold Process Soap Recipe

What you'll quickly learn is that you can produce your soap formulas from scratch. All you need is a few basic instructions, and you can make your blends using your favorite oils and additives. In this portion, we've provided you with three simple soap formulations that you can create and change if you choose to feel comfortable once. You can make almost any soap you want from these simple formulas.

Following the essential recipes, you can find a range of soaps that have been made for different uses and tastes. In some aspects, each of them has been designed off one of the essential recipes. You may make beautiful soaps with one of these recipes, or use them as an inspiration to create your unique formula bars.

Core Formula #1: Simple Vegetable Soap

This core recipe is designed to give you everything you want in a bar soap. The latter is warm, and it is gentle and soothing. High bar for every form of skin, including susceptible skin. Yields 15-20 soap bars weighing 5 ounces.

Ingredients:

250g coconut oil

500 g palm oil

500 g olive oil

380 g purified water

186.25 g lye

Direction

1. Follow the instructions to produce cold-processed soaps.

2. Isolate for twenty-four hours and test for hardness every day. When the soap is solid, extract it from the molds and require it to be cured for at least two weeks before use.

Core Formula #2: No Palm Vegetable Soap

This is a long-lasting, all-purpose soap for people who enjoy not to use palm oil for environmental reasons. It can be used for skincare and home cleaning purposes. Yields 15-20 soap bars weighing 5 ounces.

Ingredients

250 g coconut oil

500 g olive oil

600 g vegetable shortening

400 g distilled water

197 g lye

Instructions

1. Follow the instructions to produce cold, processed soaps.

2. Isolate for twenty-four hours and test for hardness every day. When the soap is solid, extract it from the molds and require it to be cured for at least two weeks before use.

Basic Formula #3: Simple Animal Fat Soap

This happens to be the longest-lasting, firmest, and mildest bar among the necessary formulas.

Those with sensitive skin will consider that fat animal soaps are the least harmful of soap formulations. This unique bar provides a beautiful, milky, and cooling lather that can be used anywhere from the bathroom to the kitchen and even in the laundry room. Yields 15-20 soap bars weighing 5 ounces.

Ingredients:

500 g beef stem

700 g lard

350 g distilled water

168 g lye

Instructions

1. Follow the instructions to produce cold processing soaps.

2. Isolate for twenty-four hours and test for hardness every day. When the soap is solid, extract it from the molds and require it to be cured for at least two weeks before use.

Rosebud Bundt

Wonderfully perfumed with increased geranium and also a mix of vital oils, and also naturally colored with pink clay, this feminine soap cake is excellent for a hen event or infant shower. Include a thrive of rosebuds and even a classic cake stand, and you will have an actual group pleaser.

You will need to make a 2.2 kg (4lb 9oz) soap cake.

Base Ingredients.

- 850g (1lb 14oz) olive pomace oil.

- 425g (15oz) coconut oil.

- 425g (15oz) hand oil.

- 530ml (18 1/4 fl oz) filtered water.

- 240g (8 3/4 oz) salt hydroxide (caustic soft drink).

Botanicals.

- 85g (3oz) pink clay.

- 40g (1 1/2 oz) climbed geranium essential oil - 10g (1/4 oz) lavender crucial oil.

- 10g (1/4 oz) palmarosa necessary oil - 5g (1/8 oz) vetiver critical oil.

- Rosebuds to enhance.

Tools

- 2.2 kg (4lb 9oz) attractive silicone bundt mold.

- Round cake tin.

- Necessary equipment and also devices (see Soap-Making Essentials)

1. Grease your silicone bundt mold and place it inside a rounded cake box, slightly much shorter than the elevation of the frame, and packed out below to sustain it.

2. Using greaseproof (wax) paper, eliminated a design template of the top of the mold and afterward deleted the opening in the center. Place it to one side.

3. Weigh out the oils right into the frying pan and divide off sufficient fluid oil to make a sloppy, lump-free blend when integrated with the pink clay.

4. Comply with the basic soap-making instructions until you have gotten to a light trace. Then, add the pink clay to the mixture and include the essential oils. Blend to integrate extensively and trace the oil.

5 Pour into the mold, put the pre-cut greaseproof paper cover on the surface of the soap then shield (see Cold Process).

6 Once the soap has actually hardened and also cooled, chill the mold in the freezer for an hr and afterward eliminate the bundt from the shape.

7. Decorate each slice with pink rosebuds.

8 Leave the soap cake to completely dry for 24 hrs then reduced it right into equivalent pieces using a big blade 9 Leave the soap cake to dry for a more four to six weeks, taking out the slices to allow the air to flow around them.

Technique Tip

Use a cardboard box to support the silicone and soap if you do not have a cake tin of the best dimension

If they are used on their very own, molds can be floppy.

Peppermint Pumice

Sometimes you require a get up in the morning, and this stimulating peppermint soap is guaranteed to do simply that! With fresh, tingly peppermint, a caffeine hit of cocoa and a body-polishing dosage of pumice to exfoliate and rejuvenate, all your detects are sure to be restored. This minty masterpiece will be a good favorite with the guys in your life.

You will need to make 1.8 kg (4lb) of soap

Base Ingredients

- 600g (1lb 5oz) olive pomace oil

- 300g (10½ oz) coconut oil - 300g (10½ oz) hand oil - 375ml (13fl oz).

Filtered water.

- 168g (5¾ oz) salt hydroxide (caustic soft drink).

Botanicals.

- 24g (1oz) peppermint essential oil.

- 30g (1oz) cacao powder.

- 30g (1oz) ground pumice powder.

Tools

- A proper mold to hold around 1.8 kg (4lb) of soap – Basic devices and tools (see Soap-Making Essentials)

1 Follow the standard soapmaking instructions (see Cold Process), taking approximately 90-- 120ml.

(6-- 8 tbsp) of the cozy oils out to mix the chocolate powder, pumice, and peppermint oil right into a careless mixture to avoid swellings.

2 Once trace is reached, include the blended botanicals and combine well.

3 Pour the soap right into your mold and insulate well (see Cold Process).

4 Leave the soap to dry completely. Reduced it right into rough chunks once it is unmoulded a truly rustic coating (see Cutting and Curing Cold Process Soap).

Pumice.

Pumice is a preferred botanical mostly used in soap-making for its gentle polishing capability. It is derived from ground volcanic rocks and is more often made use of in the form of rocks to scrub tough skin on the feet. These rocks are then ground into a powder form, which serves as a superb exfoliant when contributed to soap, gentle enough for use on the face in addition to the body.

Cacao Powder.

Cacao powder is widely made use of in baking, but it is also made use of effectively in cold process soap-making as an all-natural colorant. It is favored for its beautiful abundant brown color and even the subtle scent that it gives to the soap. Matched with vanilla scent, it offers an abundant earthy aroma and also tone.

Soothing Face Soap

With a foundation of wax, this soap is a soft soap to be used on fragile facial skin.

Shea butter, oatmeal, and lavender add additional calming and softening properties to this slightly fragrant yet medicinal bowl. Yields 15-20 soap bars weighing 5 ounces.

Ingredients:

300 g beef tallow

350 g olive oil

70 g castor oil

100 g shea butter

50 g ground oatmeal

25 g dried lavender, finely ground

225 g purified water

111 g lye

Instructions

1. Follow the instructions to produce cold processing soaps.

2. Attach the dried lavender and the oatmeal to the remnants of the wash.

3. Isolate for twenty-four hours and test for hardness every day. When the soap is solid, extract it from the molds and require it to be cured for at least two weeks before use.

Kitchen and Bath Hand Soap

This huge lathering soap combines beeswax and olive oil to maintain the skin moist and clean while the application of brewed coffee serves as an odor remover that is ideal for eliminating the scent of dried food from your mouth. It yields 15-20 inches of soap bars.

Ingredients:

250 g coconut oil

500 g palm oil

600 g olive oil

150 g castor oil

50 g beeswax

440 g cold-brewed coffee made with distilled water 219 g lye

Di

1. Follow the instructions to produce cold processing soaps.

2. When the soap traces, apply the beeswax.

3. Isolate for twenty-four hours and test for hardness every day. When the soap is solid, extract it from the molds and require it to be cured for at least two weeks before use.

Lavender Heaven

The fantastic recipe is loved by many because of its magical fragrance. Follow the steps in cold process soap-making steps. Add the required ingredients under "the magic touch" at trace. Allow your wonder soap cure for 3-4 weeks. Add colorants if you desire. The blend of patchouli together with the lavender and orange essence gives this recipe a distinctive touch This recipe makes about 3 pounds of lavender

The Essential oils

- Coconut oil (10.2 ounces)
- Olive oil (10.2 ounces)
- Sunflower oil (3.4 ounces)
- Cocoa butter (1.7 ounces)
- Castor oil (1.7 ounces)
- Palm oil (6.8 ounces)

For the Lye solution

4.9 ounces of lye

11.3 ounces of water

The magic touch

2 tbsp. of lightly ground lavender buds 0.8 ounces of lavender essential oil 0.5 ounces of orange essential oil 0.3 ounces of patchouli essential oil

All-Purpose Shower and Bath Bar

This soap provides a robust and smooth lather while the milk of the goat and the shea butter are extra moisturizing. This bar is ideal for use on the entire body, including the neck, head, and even as a shaving bar in the bathroom. Earl Gray tea blended offers the bar a soft fragrance and a bright tint. Yields 15-20 soap bars weighing 5 ounces.

Ingredients

300 g coconut oil

300 g palm oil

550 g olive oil

150 g castor oil

100 g shea butter

25 g dried lavender, finely ground

2 oz lavender essential oil

6 oz goat milk

1 oz earl gray tea

412 g distilled water

206 g lye

Instructions

1. Steep the Earl Gray tea in 22.0 g of the distilled water used.

2. The milk of the goat should be cooled to the right condition.

3. Follow the instructions to produce cold processing soaps.

4. Add the juice of the goat to the oils once the oils exceed a temperature of 110 ° F/43 ° C.

5. Earl Gray tea, ground lavender, and lavender essential oil should be applied to the residue.

6. Isolate for twenty-four hours and test for hardness every day. When the soap is solid, extract it from the molds and require it to be cured for at least two weeks before use.

Basic Face and Shave Bar

This face and shave bar provides a robust lather while the castor oil adds extra glycerine to the soap. This, coupled with the glide produced by the clay, and the soothing and moisturizing properties of beeswax and shea butter, creates a smooth, moisturizing soap that will soothe your face and body even after shaving. Yields 15-20 soap bars weighing 5 ounces.

Ingredients

200 g coconut oil

300 g vegetable shortening

400 g olive oil

150 g castor oil

40 g bentonite clay (add to trace)

25 g beeswax

100 g shea butter

336 g distilled water

167 g lye

Instructions

1. Follow the instructions to produce cold processing soaps.

2. Isolate for twenty-four hours and test for hardness every day. When the soap is solid, extract it from the molds and require it to be cured for at least two weeks before use.

Masculine Face and Shave Bar

A shave bar mainly designed for men, coconut oil, castor oil, and IPA produces a substantial, thick lather. Hemp oil provides a sweet, nutty oil, but it also provides a moisturizing and restorative aspect that is rich in vitamins and heals the skin. The clay provides a glide that helps your shaver to move effortlessly across your face.

Hops are softening of facial hair and also have antibacterial properties, which stops the healing of any tiny nicks or abrasions that may occur. Yields 15-20 soap bars weighing 5 ounces.

Ingredients

300 g beef tallow

300 g olive oil

150 g coconut oil

150 g castor oil

200 g hemp oil

100 g shea butter

25 g liquid vitamin and 50 g bentonite clay

25 g fresh ground hops

342 g IPA (beer)

170 g lye

Instructions:

In this recipe, alcohol substitutes water. With best results, put the beer in a large mason jar a day or two before producing the wash. A few times a day, shake the bottle, and, as soon as the foam settles down, open it gently and remove the lid for thirty minutes to an hour.

This will remove the carbonation of the brew. Too much carbonation may pose a risk during the soap making process, so it is better to remove it as much as possible. Many soap manufacturers prefer to cook off alcohol in water, which will also minimize carbonation, but this is not necessary as long as you use a product with regular alcohol content.

1. Follow the instructions to produce cold-pressed soaps.

2. Apply vitamin E, bentonite clay, and hop to the trail.

3. Isolate for twenty-four hours and test for hardness every day. When the soap is solid, extract it from the molds and require it to be cured for at least two weeks before use.

COUNTRY PANTRY SOAP

A quick, natural soap crafted from traditional oils that can be found in any small grocery store or country pantry. There was no need for any luxury here and no outside vendors. Such oils make an excellent refrigerated bar of soap. It yields 15-20 inches of soap bars.

Ingredients

850 g lard

250 g mash oil

500 g olive oil

250 g canola oil

506 g purified water

252 g lye

Instructions

1. Follow the instructions to produce cold-processed soaps.

2. Isolate for twenty-four hours and test for hardness every day. When the soap is solid, extract it from the molds and require it to be cured for at least two weeks before use.

Herbal Shampoo Bar

This is another illustration of how to use one of the simple recipes to make a customized soap to meet your needs. Hemp and jojoba oils help to strengthen the hair. Hops are used for their famous hair fragrance, and rosemary tends to soothe the sore scalp and keeps the skin from drying out—yields 15 to 20 pins.

Ingredients

250 g coconut oil

300 g palm oil

500 g olive oil

100 g hemp seed oil

75 g jojoba oil

1-ounce lavender essential oil

1-ounce rosemary essential oil

Two teaspoons ground hops

360 g distilled water

176 g lye

Instructions

1. Put the ground hops in a tea ball or infuser and create a tea infusion of hops and distilled water. Allow the trips to steep for twenty-four hours. Cut the ground hops from the tea bag and set aside.

2. Follow the instructions to produce cold processing soaps.

3. Attach the retained field hops, lavender essential oil, and rosemary essential oil.

3. Isolate for twenty-four hours and test for hardness every day. When the soap is solid, extract it from the molds and require it to be cured for at least two weeks before use.

Invigorating Foot Soap

This citrus soap is soft with a milky lather to help soothe the feet. Added coffee is a gentle exfoliant. This bar leaves your feet warm, smooth, and refreshed. Yields 15-20 soap bars weighing 5 ounces.

Ingredients:

300 g beef tallow

150 g shea butter

50 g beeswax

400 g olive oil

100 g avocado oil

Two teaspoons ground coffee

One teaspoon orange zest

One teaspoon lemon zest

One teaspoon lime zest

315 g purified water

154.25 g lye

Instructions

1. Follow the instructions to produce cold processing soaps.

2. Attach the ground coffee, the orange zest, the lemon zest, and the lime zest.

2. Isolate for twenty-four hours and test for hardness every day. When the soap is solid, extract it from the molds and require it to be cured for at least two weeks before use.

Melt and Pour Soaps

Here you'll find some incredibly simple suggestions for personalizing melt and pour glycerin soap bases. You may note that these recipes are provided in volume measurements rather than in weight measurements used to make cold-pressed soaps. This is because, with the melting and pouring of detergent, you are not relying on the chemical reaction to the production of soap. Therefore, the measuring units do not need to be as precise.

While these recipes encourage you, the fact is that the sky is the limit to melting and pouring soaps. Let your imagination run wild. As a side note, we haven't included any rebatch or hand-milled recipes in this book, as they depend heavily on what sort of soap you're using to rebatch and the ingredients that already exist. You can also change any of the melted ingredients and spill them into a hand-milled soap.

Her Shave Soap

This is a very mild shave soap with the tendency to create a smooth, dense, vibrant, and moisturizing lather. The glycerin and the honey support the flesh, and the clay gives the skin a good glide. This soap is soft and refrigerated enough to be used for routine shaving purposes. Yields 15-20 soap bars weighing 5 ounces.

Ingredients:

400 g beef tallow

400 g olive oil

75 g jojoba oil

100 g shea butter

100 g wheat germ oil

50 g bentonite clay

30 g honey

1-ounce chamomile essential oil

1-ounce lavender essential oil

330 g purified water

163.25 g lye

Instructions

1. Follow the instructions to produce cold processing soaps.

2. Remove glycerin, bentonite clay, sugar, chamomile essential oil, and lavender essential oil.

3. Isolate for twenty-four hours and test for hardness every day. When the soap is solid, extract it from the molds and require it to be cured for at least two weeks before use.

Chocolate-Covered Fruit Bar

This bar is absolutely decadent and so mouth-watering that you'll need reminders not to consume it! Available up to four bars depending on the size and form of your molds.

Ingredients

2 cups heat and mix base wash,

1/4 cup condensed milk

One teaspoon cocoa powder

One tablespoon candied orange peel, sliced.

Ten drops of sweet orange essential oil

Five drops of peppermint essential oil

Instructions:

1. Follow the instructions for melting and pouring wash.

Melt and Pour Tropical Oasis Bar

This bar can carry you to the tropical oasis of your dreams. Laced with pineapple, lemon, and jasmine, this makes the perfect summertime bar. Up to about four bars, depending on the size and form of your molds.

Ingredients:

2 cups heat and spray base wash,

1/4 cup grated almonds,

1/4 cup finely ground crushed coconut,

One teaspoon lime zest

10 drops lime essential oil

5 drops jasmine essential oil

Instructions:

1. Follow the instructions for melting and pouring wash.

Simple Exfoliating Bar

This bar is a suitable example of how you can use a fast melt and pour base to transform it into a personalized spa bar. Gently wipe the exfoliants away from dry skin, and the caffeine invigorates and soothes. Up to four rings, depending on the size and form of your molds.

Ingredients:

2 cups of molten soap base

½ cup of grated almond base

Two teaspoons of finely ground coffee base

15-20 drops of sweet orange essential oil

Instructions:

1. Follow the instructions for melt and pour wash.

Plant Mint Bar

This soothing mint bar is an excellent reminder of a new herbal plant. This type of bar makes a unique soap for both hot and colder climates, with the inclusion of calming powdered milk. Up to four bars, depending on the actual size and form of your molds.

Ingredients:

2 cups heat and spray base soap

½ cup condensed milk

½ cup dried mint leaves, finely ground

10 drops peppermint essential oil

5 drops rosemary essential oil

Instructions:

1. Follow the instructions for melt and pour wash

Basic Moisturizing Soap Recipe

This lovely mixture of gentle oils allows a mild soap that leaves the skin clean and smooth.

Ingredients

24 oz. Distilled Water

9 oz. Sodium hydroxide

17 oz Coconut Oil

16 oz. Safflower Oil

20 oz. Palm Oil

8 oz. Olive Oil

3 oz. Sweet Almond Oil

Sweet Shower Bar

This bar is a beautiful gift to the men in your life, or to anyone who likes a more earthy and sweet, fragrant soap. Honey and powdered milk are moisturizing, and the spices are calming and relaxing. This produces roughly four bars depending on the size and form of your molds.

Ingredients

2 cups melt and spray soap foundation,

1/4 cup powdered milk

Two teaspoons honey

One teaspoon ground sage

One teaspoon dried basil

Two teaspoons of fresh rosemary, ground

5 drops cinnamon essential oil

10 drops rosemary essential oil

Instructions:

1.   Follow the instructions for melt and pour wash.

Aloe Vera Soap

Aloe Vera is the most popular herb used in skincare. It includes about 20 amino acids, minerals such as calcium, magnesium, and sodium in sufficient quantities, enzymes, vitamins, polysaccharides, nitrogen and other components that make it a marvelous plant.

14.9 oz coconut oil

13.4 oz olive oil

10.5 oz lard

2.5 oz shea butter

9.6 oz aloe gel and water purée (add water to aloe until a minimum of 9.6 oz)

6.7 oz lye (NaOH)

9.9 oz water

Follow ordinary soap producing procedures:

1. Carefully attach leek to the water and heat the oils until they are molten while it cools.

2. When the temperature is about the same, apply the lye mixture to the oils

3. First, use the aloe gel in front of the line. Blend well until the mixture thickens to a small level.

4. Pour into the mold, insulate and require to be set for 24 to 48 hours.

5. Unmold, cut and steam the soaps for at least four weeks.

Note: If you use aloe from your plant, make sure you use only a transparent gel from the seeds.

Sweet Honey Bar

You should apply natural ingredients such as honey, wheat germ, and oatmeal to your melt and pour soap base to make a soap that looks, tastes, and smells like an elegant luxury bar. Approximately four bars of soap are produced depending on the size and form of your container.

Ingredients:

2 cups melt and spray soap base

Two teaspoons beeswax pellets

Two tablespoons honey

One tablespoon wheat germ

One tablespoon oatmeal, finely ground

10 drops bergamot essential oil

Instructions

1. Follow the instructions for melt and pour soap.

Beeswax Soap

Beeswax is a legitimate product of nature that we would have to owe the honey bees credit: it takes about ten pounds of honey to produce a pound of beeswax! Beeswax has been used throughout history for a variety of purposes and niches, from portraits to paschal candles.

Now, there are several applications of beeswax that could be encased in a bath. It is known to seal in moisture right inside the skin and can also keep the skin supple and soft. You might say good-bye to a dried or cracked skin. It also has the capacity to coat the surface with a covering when applied.

Beeswax covers the skin and avoids damage to the environment. Antibacterial and anti-inflammatory are some of the inherent properties of wax.

Beeswax has the natural healing powers of honey. It renders beeswax a strong rash soother in soap and could fix skin problems. It also gives it a therapeutic supplement because bacteria-fighting is a critical step in preventing more exacerbation and inflammation of the skin. Because it has minimal pain and allergenic risk, it is healthy to use. It may be suggested for those who have sensitive skin and those who are not connected to the counter with chemically based goods. Pores are not clogged, which is also a protective measure.

Blocked pores contribute to the accumulation of oils and debris in the skin, causing inflammation and infection.

Ingredients

4 oz almond oil

6 oz canola oil

8 oz coconut oil

7 oz olive oil

6 oz soya oil

1-ounce beeswax

4.3 oz lye (NaOH)–8 percent superfast

12 oz water

2 tbsp. Honey

Heat oils up to 150 ° F. Add the wax (you can brush it, chunk it, pre-melt it).

Heat to 115 degrees F. Lye and bath at around 110 ° F.

Attach the lee/water to the fats, attach the honey to the soft residue.

Stir until well mixed.

Do not spill more than one inch deep.

 Protect with a Saran style cover that removes soda ash).

Don't cover yourself with a pillow, just place a cookie sheet over the end.

Avocado Soap

Avocado has many advantages for the flesh, whether it is consumed or used topically.

The oil has almost the same properties as the berries, such as healthy fats (like omega 3), phytonutrients, and vitamins A, D, and E.

It is also rich in minerals, particularly potassium, which allows the skin to penetrate uniformly, quickly, and more profound than most other oils, rendering the skin smooth and moisturized.

The use of avocado oil for soap making improves the drying properties of your finished product and brings creaminess to the soap lather.

Ingredients

33 percent avocado oil

30 percent palm oil

30 percent palm kernel oil

7 percent sweet almond oil

Rosemary Oleoresin Extract (ROE)

Lye (NaOH)

Distilled or Mineral Water

Avocado Pure Rosemary Oleoresin Extract (ROE) is a pure antioxidant extract that efficiently increases the shelf life of your oils and combats oxidation in your homemade soaps. You only need a small amount-between 0.02 percent and 0.05 percent PPO. So you'd need between .2 and .5 grams of ROE per 1,000 grams of oil (a little over 2 lbs.).

Avocado Puree: The use of avocado puree helps to significantly reduce the amount of bubbles you get in your lather. To stop that, raising the superfast to 3%. That's going to help you get a rich, creamy lather to hold some of the bubbles contained in it.

The most crucial point here is to ensure that your avocado flesh is very soft.

Use your stick mixer in a small bowl and filter until all the bumps are gone, and it's 100% smooth. Attach the purée of avocado to the oils in a thin trace and blend until thoroughly mixed.

Since the major part of your puree is water, you should substitute half the amount of water with puree.

Instructions:

Run a formula using a lye calculator to find out a lot of each product you need for a given amount of soap. E.g., if you want to make a small test batch of 1 pound at 3 percent superfast, you'd need the following:

Put the recipe through a lye calculator and figure out the quantity of each product you'll need for a certain amount of soap. For example, to make a small test batch of 1 pound at 3% superfat, you'd need the following.

5.28 oz avocado oil

4.8 palm oil

4.8 palm kernel oil

1.12 sweet almond oil

2.311 lye (NaOH)

6.08 oz total liquid (3.04 oz water + 3.04 oz avocado puree)

0.7 oz ROE essential oil of preference (optional)

1. Begin by linen your soap mold and weigh your ingredients.

Prepare the purée of avocado; make sure there are no clumps. It's ok to do more than you're going to need.

2. Carefully transfer the lye to the water (we only use half the amount of water as the other half will be added later in the form of avocado pure). Set aside to cool down.

3. Warm the oils in the pan until they are molten, add the purée of avocado, ROE, and blend well.

4. When both the lye water solution and the oils are about 125-135 degrees, slowly pour the lye water into your oils, stirring all the way.

Use a stick-blender on the spurts to combine correctly.

5. Remove the essential oil (if used) and mix until the soap hits a soft trace.

6. Pour the mixture into the mold and let it sit for about twenty-four to forty-eight hours. Once the soap has dried enough, unmold it, cut it and make it cure in a well-ventilated area (preferably a cookie rack) for four weeks.

Bamboo Charcoal Soap

Bamboo charcoal powder is known for its skincare advantages in Asia. It's perfect to use with any skin, but ultimately heaven for oily skin!

The carbon dioxide solution removes contaminants, impurities, and waste fat by digging deep into the pores. This softly exfoliates the skin without leaving any traces behind, and its anti-bacterial and anti-fungal effects render this suitable for anyone suffering from acne, psoriasis, and eczema.

When in contact with water, carbon dioxide powder releases several beneficial minerals, such as calcium, potassium, and magnesium, producing a cooling, soothing hot spring-water effect.

Push this formula through a lye converter and figure out how much lye, water, and oil you're going to need for a certain quantity of soap.

Ingredients

9.6 oz palm oil

8 oz olive oil

8 oz coconut oil

4.8 oz palm kernel oil

1.6 oz castor oil

12.1 oz water

4.7 oz lye (NaOH)

One tablespoon bamboo charcoal powder

Follow regular cold process procedures. Combine the charcoal powder with a small amount of hot oil until it is completely dissolved, and add the remaining oils in a thin trace. Palm kernel oil can render the mark quicker, so be careful.

Castile Soap

Castile soap is the term used in English-speaking countries for olive oil soap manufactured in a similar style to that developed in the Castile region of Spain. It is an all-vegetable soap made primarily from olive oil, although sometimes it may also contain small quantities of other vegetable oils, such as banana, coconut, hemp, and jojoba.

This recipe uses 100% olive oil, which allows for a very sweet, low sweating, a horizontal bar that can be used both on the body and on the neck. It's perfect for all skin types, mainly dry, sensitive and mature skin. It could even be used for children.

Due to the high content of olive oil, this soap can take longer to reach its mark, so make sure to use a blender. It will also take longer to recover (at least six weeks). Make sure the soap remains fresh between the showers or melts quickly. The formula provided below is produced with 32 ounces of oil/fat to make 2 pounds of soap.

- 32 oz olive oil (generic olive oil fits best)
- 4.07 oz lye
- 12.16 oz distilled water
- 1/2 or 1 oz soap healthy scent product Using typical cold process methods.

Coconut Soap

Coconut oil is one of the most widely used oils in cold soap production, along with olive oil. It's also incredibly popular among natural beauty blogs and DIYers because of its incredible skin properties.

But there are two approaches to blend coconut-derived ingredients into homemade soaps. Also, there is another coconut commodity that is a little underused in soap making: coconut milk.

Ingredients

- 25 percent Palm Oil
- 25 percent Sweet Almond Oil
- 20 percent Coconut Oil
- 20 percent Olive Oil
- 5 percent Castor Oil
- 5 percent Coconut Butter
- Lye (NaOH)
- Coconut Milk

Go to your preferred lye calculator and run the numbers. Using 5% superfat and substitute the water with coconut milk, just as you would for goat milk.

Since coconut milk doesn't seem to "heat" at high temperatures, certain people will blend it directly with lee. However, just to be on the safe side of it, some people like to use it as hard as they can.

Floral Soap

This soap is filled with the healing properties of flower petal oils: fundamental, distilled, and fixed— perfect for extra sensitive and dry skin. It is scented with an elegant, feminine mix of jasmine and rose.

Ingredients

42 percent heavy oleic sunflower oil, blended with calendula, lavender and chamomile buds and petals

20 percent coconut oil,

76 degree

19 percent babassu oil

7 percent shea butter

7 percent rosehip oil

Evening primrose oil (5 percent)

0.5 to 0.7 oz PPO (Per Pound of Oil)

The mix of jasmine and rose essential oil

For a small sample of 1 pound at 5 percent superfast, add the essential oils to the trace; insulate, unmold after 24 to 48 hours and leave to cure for about four weeks before use.

Cucumber Soap

Cucumber juice has, for a long time, been used as an astringent facewash and acts as a gentle washing agent and skin toner in these recipes.

- 1 and 1/2 c. Clear tallow
- 1 c. pulp of cucumber
- 1/2 c. Vegetable oil
- 3/4 c. Hot and hot drinking
- 1/4 c. Lee flakes.
- 1/2 tsp. Vitamin E oil or Wheat germ oil (external use)
- Two drops of clove EO (optional)

Cut and grind cucumber until very small. Melt fat and add up the cucumber—heat for half an hour or a couple of hours on the back of the woodstove. The pulp contributes small greenish-yellow specks to the soap.

Remove the fat then set aside to cool down. Stir the leek flakes in cold water until dissolved and set aside to cool. Prepare the oil properly with petroleum jelly.

When the fat and the lees are dry, slowly add the lees to the fat, stirring constantly.

Keep mixing until the paste is thick and creamy. Apply wheat germ oil or vitamin E oil, add a drop or two of clove oil, beat well, and spread evenly.

Pour in the molds.

Approximate yieldd: 1 & 1/2 lbs.

CUCUMBER SOAP II

- 15 oz sunflower oil
- 30 oz coconut oil
- 27 oz olive oil
- 21 oz palm oil
- 5 oz shea butter
- 18 oz cucumber juice (juicer fits perfectly)
- Water (19 oz)
- 14.1 oz lye (NaOH)

Extract juice from the cucumbers and add in until you have 18 oz of milk. Place this in a little reservoir and set aside.

While the oils and lyes are cooling, apply the coloring, and the picked essential oil to the pitcher with the cucumber juice in it, mix well and set aside again.

Now go back and add the lye water to your oils and mix until the trace becomes white.

That's when you add the cucumber bowl, E.O. Then coloring, then finish blending until you have a little of it, then add it.

French Rose Clay Soap

Rose clay also provides silkiness, slide, and shower absorbency. It is very gentle and can, therefore, be used comfortably with common, responsive, and advanced skin types.

Ingredients

30 percent olive oil

30 percent coconut oil

15 percent apricot kernel oil

10 percent castor oil

10 percent cocoa butter

5 percent jojoba oil

Two teaspoons PPO (per pound of oils)

Run this formula through a lye calculator such as soap calc to get the exact level or measurement of the volume of soap you want to create.

Follow the standard soap making techniques and use the light traced clay.

Another alternative is to apply it directly to the soap mixture for exfoliating, speckled soap. And, for a more consistent bath, set aside a little of the hot oils and remove the clay entirely before applying the slurry back to the remaining soap mixture.

Ingredients

4.8 oz olive oil

4.8 oz coconut oil

2.4 oz apricot kernel oil

1.6 oz castor oil

1.6 oz cocoa butter

0.8 oz jojoba oil

Two teaspoons French rose clay

6.08 oz diluted or demineralized water

2.226 oz lye (NaOH)

You can scent your soap with an essential oil blend of rose geranium, jasmine, ylang-ylang and sandalwood (0.5 oz lye)

You can insulate and have a cut once the soap is strong enough (between 24h and 48h). Let it cure on a cooling rack for about four weeks.

Green Clay Soap

Green clay soap assists with mild break-ups, redness, and inflammation. This removes contaminants and impurities and produces skin-nourishing minerals such as calcium, potassium, silicon, and copper.

Ingredients

30 percent olive oil

30 percent babassu oil

23 percent avocado oil

7 percent castor oil

10 percent shea butter

Green clay (2 percent)

0.5 oz PPO eucalyptus and lemongrass essential oil blend.

Run this formula through your preferred lye calculator to get the exact measurement of the volume of soap you want to create.

4.8 oz olive oil

4.8 oz babassu oil

3.68 oz avocado oil

1.12 oz castor oil

1.6 oz shea butter

Lye (2.209 oz)

6.08 oz demineralized distilled or water

0.5 oz essential oils (NaOH)

Green clay (0.32 oz)

0.5 oz. essential oils

You're going to end up with a soap full of beautiful small spices.

Set aside a part of the hot oils for even, consistent soaps and substitute the mud, mixing well until there are no clumps or lumps. Instead, add this slurry to the soft trace mixture of the wash.

Isolate overnight with an old towel or pillow and unmold after 24 to 48 hours.

Cut the mixture into bits and let it recover for about four weeks on a cooling rack.

Honey Soap

Honey has been used for skin care for decades, thanks to its moisturizing and antibacterial qualities. The formula below allows for a very lathering soap bar that leaves the skin smooth and moisturized.

- 48 percent beef tallow, developed
- 25 percent olive oil
- 20 percent coconut oil,
- 76degree
- 5 percent castor oil
- 2 percent beeswax
- lye (NaOH)
- diluted or demineralized water
- 4 percent essential oil mix with citronella and lemongrass (optional)
- 3 percent honey 1 pound study sample, 5 percent superfast:
- 7.68 oz beef tallow
- 4.0 oz olive oil
- 3.2 oz coconut oil

Melt the beeswax in a suitable boiler until it is liquid. Warm leftover oils and wax and mix until completely absorbed, even in texture and color.

When the lye and fats are lukewarm, slowly add the lye to the butter, mixing until thick and creamy. In a thin stream, apply the warm wax mixture and beat vigorously to spread uniformly. Add some honey and essential oils. Pour in the molds.

Remember that the honey is going to heat up and speed up the saponification process, so be ready to pour the mixture into the molds rapidly.

Do not insulate and place the soap in the freezer overnight to avoid overheating. Acrylic and silicone molds are better suited to this recipe, as wooden log molds retain more heat.

Indigo Antiseptic Soap

This is a pure antiseptic soap with essential oil for lavender and peppermint. The vibrant blue color is obtained from natural indigo powder. True indigo is a natural dye used by ancient civilizations in Egypt, India, Mesopotamia, and Asia.

Ingredients

16.91 oz coconut oil

13.53 oz rice bran oil

3.38 oz sesame oil

4.5 oz lye (NaOH)

10.48 oz distilled water or rainwater

1/2 oz indigo paste or powder

1/2 oz peppermint essential oil

1/2 oz lavender essential oil

Regular cold storage procedures. This contains around 3.2 pounds of soap.

Whether you prefer to make a more substantial (or smaller) amount, you can turn the formula into percentages. Using soap calc (or another lye converter of your choice) to get the specific amounts you need for a specified batch size.

- 50 percent coconut oil

- 10 percent sesame oil
- 1 tsp PPO peppermint essential oil
- 40 percent rice bran oil
- 1 tsp PPO indigo paste or powder (about 4.2 g)
- 1 tsp PPO lavender essential oil PPO= per pound of

Mocha Soap

This recipe makes a soap bar that turns out thick, smooth, and very rich. The faint scent of coffee and chocolate makes you want to consume it.

- 25 percent coconut oil
- 25 percent palm oil
- 25 percent palm kernel oil
- 12.5 percent cocoa butter
- 12.5 percent grape seed oil
- double-dip coffee
- cocoa powder (approximately 1 tsp per pound of soap).

You would need to pass the formula through a lye calculator to get the exact numbers you need for a given amount of soap.

For starters, to make a small batch of 1 pound at 5 percent, superfast, soap calc offers me the following:

- 4 oz coconut oil
- 4 oz palm oil
- 4 oz palm kernel oil
- 2 oz cocoa butter
- 2 oz grapeseed oil
- 2,4 oz lye (NaOH)
- 6 oz double-strength coffee
- 1 tsp cocoa powder

Instructions

Melt oils and apply lye to double-strength coffee. Place some of the hot oils in a separate container— just enough to combine the cocoa powder until it is fully diluted (you don't want to end up with clumps in your soap).

Add the lye to the oils and combine them with a stick blender. Attach the cocoa powder mixture to a soft trace and blend until smooth. Pour into the mold, cover it in a blanket and let it rest for 48 hours. Unmold, cut into bars and leave to cure for at least four weeks in a cookie rack in a well-ventilated room.

Sea Salt Soap

Sea salts have many advantages for the skin. Not only do they eliminate contaminants from the body and reduce inflammation, but they also provide other skin nutrients such as magnesium, zinc, calcium, potassium, and iodine.

A powerful combination of minerals tends to calm muscles and skin while increasing blood circulation. Salt soaps are not dried, contrary to what many people believe. Sea salt is excellent for soothing skin tissue and maintaining hydration, successfully managing heat, and reducing water retention.

These salt bars are a bit tricky— you've got to cut them as soon as they cool, often still soft because they're going to turn rock hard and crumbly, making it hard to cut.

Though standard sea salt is being used for this recipe, but you can use any kind of salt you choose, including the beautiful pink Himalayan salt. The only spice you're not allowed to use is Dead Sea Salt. It absorbs too much moisture from the air to render the soap sweat. So you'd best save those for body scrubs.

Using fine ground salt for clean, softly exfoliating soap — optionally sprinkle the top of the raw soap with coarse salt over a beautifully textured surface.

Ingredients

30 percent olive oil

30 percent coconut oil

30 percent palm kernel oil

5 percent castor oil

5 percent shea butter

7 percent sea salt

Lye (NaOH}

EO of preference (0.5 to 1 oz PPO)

Mineral or distilled water

Use a lye calculator to determine precisely how much of each product you need for a given amount of soap. For a small test sample of 1 pound at 8 percent superfast, soap calc can provide you the following:

4.8 oz olive oil

4.8 oz coconut oil

4.8 oz palm kernel oil

0.8 oz castor oil

0.8 oz shea butter

1.12 oz sea salt

2.374 oz lye

6.08 oz water

0.7 oz EO

Follow recommended soap making techniques. Next, clean the lyes: carefully attach the lyes to the water and set aside to cool.

Melt the oils and butter in an oven, and when both lye-water and oils are below 130F (and preferably within 10 degrees of each other), slowly apply the lye-water to the oils.

Blend with a stick blender or a hand blender until the trace is white. Add the essential oils and the salt until well mixed.

Pour into the jar, insulate and allow for washing for 24 to 48 hours. Once the soap has been dried, unmolded, and split. Place the cut pieces of soap on a cooling rack, ideally in a well-ventilated room, and enable them to be cured for 4 to 6 weeks.

Tea Tree Soap

Tea tree oil is obtained from the leaves of Melaleuca alternifolia, a shrubby tree native to New Zealand and Australia. It has been used for about 100 years plus in all sorts of natural products owing to its many medicinal features.

Tea tree oil is anti-fungal, antibacterial, and antiseptic, making it ideal for those with acne, oily skin, poison ivy, psoriasis, and other skin conditions.

This method blends the soft, nourishing oils-from olives, hemp, almonds, and avocado-with the healing properties of the tea tree. The effect is a quiet, clean, and soothing bar that helps regulate excess sebum and soothes acne and rashes.

- 45 percent olive oil

- 30 percent coconut oil

-13 percent sweet almond oil

-water

-lye (NaOH)

-Tea tree essential oil

Run the formula through the lye converter and find out exactly how much fat, lye, and water you need for a given amount of soap. For a small batch of one pound at 5% superfat, soap calc. gives us the following:

- 7.2 oz olive oil

- 4.8 oz coconut oil

- 2.08 oz sweet almond oil

- 1.92 oz avocado oil

- 6.08 oz water

- 2.27 oz lye

- 0.7 oz tea tree essential oil

Instructions:

1. Begin by carefully applying the lees to the water and mix until all the lees have been dissolved. While the lees cool down, they measure and heat the oils.

2. When the oils and the lye-water are about 95 degrees Fahrenheit, slowly add the lye-water to the oils and combine with a stick blender.

3. When the mixture hits a soft trace, add the fat of the tea tree (and any other essential oils that you want to use) and blend until fully incorporated. Pour in molds and insulate for 24 to 48 hours.

4. If the soap is hard enough (it may take longer depending on your environmental conditions), unmold it, cut it and let it recover in a well-ventilated area for 4 to 6 weeks.

Honey and Oat Scrub

Often soap consisting of crucial or fragrance oils can be irritating to sensitive skin, so it's great to have a skin-friendly soap such as this in your repertoire. Oats supply peeling and structure to the soap, and also honey has incredible homes. Not only is it disinfectant, however it is additionally a humectant, which attracts wetness from the air. This soap will certainly smell outstanding as soon as made and also will usually be perplexed with fudge-- don't be fooled!

You will need to make 1.8 kg (4lb) of soap.

Base Ingredients.

- 600g (1lb 5oz) olive pomace oil.

- 300g (10½ oz) coconut oil.

- 300g (10½ oz) hand oil.

- 375ml (13fl oz) filtered water.

- 168g (5¾ oz) sodium hydroxide (caustic soft drink).

Botanicals.

- 60g (2¼ oz) runny honey.

- 100g (3½ oz) rolled oats.

Equipment.

- Coffee mill or blender or food processor.

- Necessary tools and devices (see Soap-Making Essentials).

Technique Tip.

Grind fifty percent of the oats right into a more elegant structure using a coffee grinder or blender or food processor. This generates a smoother bar while still maintaining several of the rustic components of the oats.

1. Weigh out the honey and rolled oats and pop half of the oats right into a mill or blender or food processor to make them into a great powder. Put every one of the botanicals into a recipe.

2 Follow the standard soap-making guidelines (see Cold Process).

Before adding the sodium hydroxide and also water to the oils, take a couple of tablespoons of cozy oil out and incorporate it with the honey and oats to make a careless mixture.

3 Once the trace has occurred, add the honey, oats, and also oil. Combine well to make sure the added oil traces.

4 Add to your selected mold and also cover (see Cold Process). Honey can overheat, so do not also insulate a lot. Delegate dry, unmould the soap and also reduce as preferred (see Curing and reducing Cold Process Soap).

Technique Tip

When using any clays, powders, or milk, you will need to mix them with some of the oils before including them to the mapped soap. This prevents swellings of unmixed botanicals in your ended up soap, including them to the mapped soap.

Remove a section of the dissolved oils and mix with the clays or powders to make a careless mixture. Once the trace has been reached, add this combination with the other botanicals and blend to ensure the oils are well traced.

Honey

It has been used in skincare and healing for centuries and is well documented for its antibacterial and healing residential properties. And being calming and also healing it is a humectant, which indicates it attracts moisture from the air, offering honey soap its very mild cleaning power. Its combination with oats is the perfect recipe to soothe delicate skin.

Soap Style

Use bubble cover to cover the soap rather than cling movie (plastic wrap). It will leave a fascinating honeycomb pattern externally of the soap.

Shaver's Saviour

Industrial cutting foams can be extreme and also drying to the delicate skin of the face. The old-fashioned technique of damp cutting can be equally as effective and is much kinder and gentler to skin. This standard soap recipe, with the enhancement of a small quantity of castor oil, permits a lovely soap and also a good slip on the surface, helping the razor to slide. Cut the solvent right into rounds with a cookie cutter and location in a pot for usage with a cutting brush.

You will need to make 1.9 kg (4lb 3oz) of shaving foam.

Base Ingredients.

- 600g (1lb 5oz) olive pomace oil.

- 300g (10½ oz) coconut oil - 300g (10½ oz) palm oil - 75g (2¾ oz) castor oil.

- 390ml (13½ fl oz) filtered water - 177g (6oz) sodium hydroxide (caustic soda).

Botanicals.

- 60g (2¼ oz) bentonite clay - 24g (1oz) calendula oil.

- 30g (1oz) tea tree essential oil.

Tools.

- Loaf mold to hold roughly 1.9 kg (4lb 3oz) of soap - Deep round.

cookie cutter with serrated side.

- Ceramic pots (more significant than your cutter).

- Necessary tools and also tools (see Soap-Making Essentials)

1. Follow the basic soap-making instructions or guidelines (see Cold Process), taking about 120ml (8 tbsp) of the warm oils out to blend the bentonite clay, tea tree essential oil, and calendula oil into a sloppy blend to prevent lumps.

2. Once trace is reached, include the botanicals and incorporate well. Put the soap right into your mold and insulate (see Cold Process).

3. Once completely dry, slice the soap into bars or use a cookie cutter to make soaps (rounded soaps).

4. Allow the round soaps to dry for about four to six weeks completely. Finally, pop the solvent right into a pot and also use it with a shaving brush to produce a beautiful lather.

Technique Tip

Recycle an item of old drain right into a rounded mold. Cut up the sides, oil it, seal the bottom.

Put the soap in, seal the top and also keep the mold upright then adhere to launch the soap and reduce when thawed.

Organic Basics.

Bentonite clay is a green volcanic clay usually made use of in face masks to soak up oils. Calendulaoil is normally healing and soothes irritation, and tea tree essential oil has antibacterial and antifungal homes. With each other, they combine to make a terrific cut.

Pina Colada Layers.

If you like pina colada, you'll enjoy this enjoyable and fruity layered soap! Pineapple and coconut fragrances mix up to develop a tempting pina colada scent that will evoke ideas of lazy vacation nights next to the beach. By splitting the components and making two batches, you can add color and fragrance to each independently and also layer them for a striking effect.

You will need to make 1.8 kg (4lb) of soap.

Base Ingredients. Make two times for two little sets.

- 300g (10½ oz) olive pomace oil.

- 150g (5½ oz) coconut oil.

- 150g (5½ oz) palm oil.

- 187ml (6½ fl oz) water.

- 84g (3oz) salt hydroxide (caustic soda).

Botanicals.

- Batch 1:.

- 5ml (1 tsp) annatto yellow natural colorant.

- 6g (1/8 oz) pineapple fragrance.

- Batch 2:.

- 12g (3/8 oz) coconut fragrance.

- 30g (1oz) desiccated coconut.

Equipment.

- Deep mold to hold roughly 1.8 kg (4lb) of soap.

- Necessary tools and tools (see Soap-Making Essentials).

1 Carefully ration the oils and water for both sets and the botanicals.

2. Follow the basic soap-making instructions to make set one (see Cold Process).

Add the colorant and also pineapple fragrance at trace.

3. Half fill the mold and insulate well (see Cold Process).

4 Make the 2nd set quickly, adding the coconut fragrance and desiccated coconut at trace.

5 Uncover the initial batch in the mold. Promptly put the second patch over the top of the initial set to fill the cavity. Cover the soap once again and protect it well, as previously.

6. Unmould the soap, reduced it either into chunks or slices depending on the mold you were making use of and left for 4 to six weeks to treat (see cutting and Curing Cold Process Soap).

Technique Tip.

When making smaller sets, consider every little thing out ahead of time and work at the more top end of the.

Temperature range to stay clear of heat loss and its resultant problems. If you thaw the oils and make the salt hydroxide mix for the second set about 15 mins after the first, you will undoubtedly be able to make both sets rapidly without losing way too much heat.

Botanical Basics.

Dry coconut works as a gentle exfoliant. Include it to one batch to give your soap a different textured side.

Cheat's Castile Soap.

Conventional Castile soap is usually made with one hundred percent olive oil, which provides a long trace and takes a substantially very long period to dry out. If you feel that palm oil is not an active ingredient that you wish to make use of in your soap base right here is different with a massive portion of olive pomace oil and some extra beeswax and cocoa butter, which generates a hard and nourishing fragrance-free soap.

You will need to make 2kg (4lb 8oz) of soap.

Base Ingredients.

- 1kg (2lb 4oz) olive pomace oil.

- 200g (7oz) coconut oil.

- 150g (5½ oz) cocoa butter

- 50g (1¾ oz) beeswax

- 400ml (14fl oz) filtered water.

- 184g (6½ oz) salt hydroxide (caustic soft drink).

Tools

- A proper mold to hold roughly 2kg (4lb 8oz) of soap – Stamp (Lazercutz, see Suppliers) (optional) - Stick blender or food processor (optional).

- Essential tools and Equipments

Technique Tip.

This soap will take a longer time to trace, so you may want to attempt the stick blender or food processor (see Advanced Strategies).

1. Adhere to the standard soap-making guidelines (see Cold Refine), guaranteeing that you make the soap at the high end of the temperature range to maintain the beeswax from setting in the frying pan. Use the stick blender or food processor (see If preferred, Advanced Techniques).

2. Thoroughly pour the soap into your mold and insulate well (see Cold Process).

3 Unmould the soap, reduced it into rustic square portions, stamp it if wanted (see Using Stamps) and also leave it for a minimum of 6 to 8 weeks to dry (see Cutting and also Healing Cold Refine Soap).

Organic Fundamentals.

Beeswax has a higher melting factor than various other oils: a job at the more top end of the temperature level.

Scale and also maintain the oil at that temperature.

Technique Tip.

Soaps high in olive oil web content tend to be a little softer, so they need to be left for at the very least 6 to 8 weeks to dry completely.

Castile Soap.

Castile soap comes from the Castile region of Spain, although it has additionally been made in Italy and France, so its beginnings are a little questionable. Put simply, and it is soap made from pure veggie oils instead of the substandard wax that was made use of in made from pure vegetable oils instead of the substandard wax that was made use of in Britain and also some locations of France. Generally, it is made from pure olive oil, which offers a soundbar of soap that spends some time to trace and also harden. It has been used as great soap for washing and the skin for centuries. Generally, it is a hard when made use of has a lather that does not produce a lot of bubbles in comparison to soaps with blended oils, square block of eco-friendly soap that.

Goat Milk and Lavender Indulgence

Goats' milk is packed with vitamins and also is beneficial and calming to the skin.

Combined with the soothing, antibacterial residential or commercial properties and beautiful scent of lavender necessary oil, you have a soap that is flawlessly gentle and soothing for dry, weary skin. There are several means of using milk in soapmaking; you can substitute it for the water in the recipe or simply use powdered goats' milk at trace as your botanical.

You will need to make 1.8 kg (4lb) of soap.

Base Ingredients.

- 600g (1lb 5oz) olive pomace oil.

- 300g (10½ oz) coconut oil.

- 300g (10½ oz) hand oil.

- 375ml (13fl oz) filtered water.

- 168g (5¾ oz) sodium hydroxide (caustic soft drink).

Botanicals.

- 100g (3½ oz) powdered goats' milk.

- 40g (1½ oz) lavender crucial oil.

Tools.

- An appropriate mold to hold about 1.8 kg (4lb) of soap.

- Primary devices and devices (see Soap-Making Essentials).

1. Follow the standard soap-making guidelines (see Cold Process). Remember to separate roughly 120ml (8 tbsp) of warm oils to mix the goats' milk powder and lavender oil into a sloppy blend to stay clear of swellings.

2. At trace, include the botanicals and, as soon as incorporated, put right into your mold.

3. Insulate gently (see Cold Process). Entrust to dry, unmould the soap, and cut as wanted (see Curing and shaving Cold Process Soap).

Technique Tip.

Milk soaps often tend to be darker in color due to the soap burning throughout the making procedure. They can be lightened by making the soap at the reduced end of the temperature level scale and also minimizing the amount of insulation. This is recommended as soon as you have understood the first batch.

Goat Milk

Goats' milk is an optimal active ingredient for soap production. It has plenty of nurturing A, C.

E, and some B vitamins, together with amino acids, citric acid, enzymes unsaturated fatty acids and also zinc. Goats' milk soap additionally includes lactic acid, an alpha-hydroxy acid, typically contained in skin renewal items. Alpha hydroxy acid aids dismiss dead skin cells, leaving smooth brand-new cells at the hydroxide acid assists dismiss dead skin cells, leaving smooth brand-new cells at the surface area.

Strawberry Sensations.

One of the best benefits of using thaw and also put soap base is the capability to make little, designed soaps that would be difficult to achieve with the cold process strategy. This simple job makes fruity, strawberry-shaped fragrant soaps that are terrifically enjoyable as gifts and will thrill the detects. The poppy seeds add to their charm by reproducing the seeds right in the strawberries.

You will need to make 200g (7oz) of soap.

Ingredients.

- 200g (7oz) opaque thaw and pour soap base.

- Alcohol for spraying.

Botanicals.

- 1.25 ml (1/4 tsp) red fluid coloring made up with 15ml (1 tablespoon) water.

- 4g (1/8 oz) strawberry scent.

- 3g (1 tsp) poppy seeds.

Tools

- Strawberry soap mold.

- Fundamental tools and implements (see Soap Making Essentials).

1. Comply with the standard soap-making instructions (see Melt and Pour). Once the soap has melted, add the scent and color a drop at a time up until you reach the desired shade.

2. Scatter the poppy seeds right into the soap up until you more than happy with the appearance.

3. Pour the detergent into the strawberry soap molds, making use of the water technique to function out just how much soap base is required to fill the cavities (see Cold Refine). Spray the soap with alcohol to lower bubbles.

Organic Basics

Poppy seeds not only contribute to the beauty of this soap, but they also have exfoliant qualities when it used.

Messy Play.

While Cold process soap making should be limited to adults for health and wellness reasons, many tasks will encourage children to discover how to make their very own soaps and other natural products. The solvents in this area are created for children to use with the help and supervision of an adult. They are messy, loaded with all-natural components, and risk-free to generate home use or as presents. My five-year-old little girl has nothing better than making her bath soap to freshen up within the bathtub, and soap-making events are so much fun for older children that love to develop items that they can be pleased with.

Scrap-saving Soap Balls.

You will find with soap-making that you will undoubtedly have a lot of scraps, oddments, and pieces lying around from removing. Place them to good use with these beautiful herbal soap bars, which can be decorated and put into beautiful bags to make cute gifs. Children like to make these as they are squidgy, untidy, and include the use of vibrant powders, flowers, and glitter. Grownups ought to grate the soap for smaller sized children. Otherwise, they can get stuck in!

You will need to make 300g (10 1/2 oz) of soap.

Base Ingredients

- Around 300g (10 1/2 oz) of cured soap scraps - Oats.

- Skin-safe shine (optional).

Botanicals.

- Blended herbs.

- Lavender buds.

- Rose flowers.

- Spirulina powder - Cinnamon powder.

Equipment.

- Cheese grater - Bowl.

- Eggboxes.

1 Grate your scraps of healed soap into a bowl. Separate the grated soap right into 75g (2 3/4 oz) piles.

2 Add your picked botanicals to the bowls. Squash the grated soap with each other and roll it in your hands to make smooth, compact spheres of soap.

3 Roll the soap right into your chosen design; the amount you need will be your personal choice! Once the balls have been covered, leave them an eggbox to dry before use.

Technique Tip

Damp the surface of each sphere by rolling it in your damp if the herbs do not stick to the soap balls palms.

Organic Basics

You can add scent to the balls if preferred with 2.5 ml (1/2 tsp) of essential oils. Essential oils are when cold and also should be managed by grownups using handwear medical cover, which is very useful.

Soap on a Rope

It is necessary to have in mind that hand-made soap needs to be dry between usage intervals to stay clear of transforming right into a stack of mush! A soap recipe with deep ridges is ideal, or you can drop the antique path of making use of scraps to make soap on a rope.

You will need to make 300g (10½ oz) of soap.

Base Ingredients.

- Scraps of healed soap or entire bars, around 300g (10½ oz) per ball.

Botanicals.

- Dried herbs or petals for decoration (optional).

Tools

- Rope or heavy-duty string.

- Bowl.

- Cheese grater/knife.

- Chopping board.

1. Grate the scraps of healed soap into a bowl.

2. Fold the rope or string in fifty percent and link completions together to form a deal with

3. Take the grated soap and also press it around the rope, just over the. knot, to make a round shape.

Continue contributing to it till you are satisfied with the end product.

4. Decorate the soap with the use of herbs or dried petals if wanted. T can be left if you prefer to have it every day.

5. Keep the soap somewhere warm and dry to set for a few weeks before using it.

Instructions

If you have a problem sticking the soap to the rope, add a little water to the grated soap.

Toy Surprise

If you have youngsters that hesitate to go anywhere near a bar of soap, these fun toy shock bars give them an actual motivation to clean, clean, wash! Any type of age-appropriate toy can be installed into benches to supply weeks of home entertainment before launching its benefit. Being active followers of radiance and color, we are adding both to the soap for even more enjoyment!

You will need to make a 200g (7oz) quantity of soap.

Base Ingredients

- 200g (7oz) clear thaw and also pour soap base.

- 10-- 15 decreases of blue food coloring.

- Pinch of skin-safe shine (readily available from soap providers-- see Suppliers).

- Rubbing alcohol in a spray container.

Botanicals

- 4g (1/8 oz) blueberry scent.

Equipment.

- Rectangular soap mold or plastic tub that will hold roughly 200g (7oz) of soap-- use water approach (see Cold Process).

- Microwave or hob (range).

- Small toy.

You can melt the soap in the microwave in 30-second ruptures, or on the hob (stove) with a dual boiler at around 120 °C (250 °F), making sure that you do not overheat it.

2. Add the scent and skin-safe shine; after that, add the food coloring a little at a time and stir well till you are satisfied with the depth of the color.

3 Spray the toy with some quantity of alcohol and place it in the mold.

4. Pour the soap over the toy to fill up the used mold and spritz with alcohol that helps to disperse any bubbles.

5. Leave the soap to cool down for 4 to 5 hours before unmoulding and using.

Organic Basics.

Usage skin-safe shine from a reputable vendor as opposed to craft shine, which can be an irritant.

Soap Style.

To make this right into soap on a rope, stand out the knotted end of a looped trap one edge of the melted soap in the mold. As the soap dries, it will solidify around the rope.

Fizzy Fun Bath Bombs.

With the fantastic quantity of fragrances botanicals and also ingredients available and the essential degree of ability included, they are perfect for kids to make as a treat for themselves or a unique homemade gift for others.

Base Ingredients.

- 450g (1lb) bicarbonate of soda - 225g (8oz) citric acid

- Filtered water for spritzing.

Botanicals.

- Ten decreases of rose geranium vital oil - 5 declines of crucial lavender oil.

- Handful of increased petals.

- 10g (1/4 oz) cocoa butter chips.

Tools

- Beautiful haze spray container.

- Silicone molds or ice trays (1 cup)

Instructions

1. Combine the citric acid and bicarbonate of soda well in the recipe to achieve 2:1 proportion throughout.

2. Add the drops of increased geranium and also vital lavender oils and mix well, damaging down any type of lumps that show up.

3. Cut the chocolate butter chips right into tiny crumbs and include with the rose petals, mixing well to incorporate.

4. Fill the beautiful haze spray bottle with water and spray the blend two or three times, mixing swiftly to combine. Then, if the combination starts to fizzle, you spray it, stir well, and the fizzing should stop. Repeat the spraying and also mixing until you have a crumbly consistency and the combination remains when you press it together in your hand,

Technique Tip

While you can buy unique molds to make the conventional round bathroom bombs, they are not essential. Silicone cake molds, eggboxes, or even ice cube trays make thoroughly excellent substitutes.

Botanical Basics

Spray it a couple of times if the mixtures begin to dry out while you are loading the mold to dampen it once more. If the mixture becomes too wet, add extra bicarbonate of soft drink and citric acid in the 2:1 proportion and also stir well to incorporate well.

Luxurious Shampoo Bar

While any type of handcrafted soap can be used to wash your hair, there are specific oils such as castor oil and also jojoba oil, that can be used in the base recipe to aid with rinsing and the problem of the hair and scalp. Change the excess fat content of the method to make hair shampoo for different hair types (with less excess thick for greasy hair and also for dehydrated hair).

You will certainly need to make 1.3 kg (3lb) of shampoo soap.

Base Ingredients

- 450g (1lb) olive pomace oil

- 200g (7oz) coconut oil

- 200g (7oz) palm oil

- 75g (2¾ oz) castor oil

- 50g (1 3/4oz) jojoba oil

- 260ml (9¼ fl oz) filtered water

- 130g (4¾ oz) sodium hydroxide (caustic soft drink) (excess fat: 7%).

Botanicals

- 8g (¼ oz) rosemary essential oil.

- 16g (½ oz) lavender essential oil.

Tools

- A suitable mold to hold approximately 1.3 kg (3lb) of soap.

- Necessary tools and equipment (see Soap-Making Essentials).

- Follow the original soap-making recipe (see Cold Process).

Castor Oil

Castor oil is made out of the castor bean plant that is rich in fatty acids, in addition to being relaxing and readily taken in by the skin. It is made use of in shampoo bars because it draws dampness from the air and also produces a luxurious conditioning soap. It attracts wetness from the sky and also creates a luxurious conditioning soap. It is often used in hot oil curing, where it coats the hair shaft and seals in dampness.

Homemade Orange Vinegar.

Self-made orange vinegar scents charming is natural to make and also can be used as both a recipe washer rinse help and a cleaning device conditioner. If you have lots of oranges, this recipe is suitable; simply add the orange halves to the jar as you use them in time.

Base Ingredients.

To make 1-- 2 liters (1 3/4-- 3 1/2 pints) of orange vinegar.

1-- 2 liters (1 3/4-- 3 1/2 pints) of white vinegar.

12-- 15 squeezed oranges (made use of fifty percent, after pressing).

Tools

- Large Kilner container.

1 Half fill a large Kilner container with white vinegar, and also, as you use your oranges, add the used fifty percent to the vinegar until the jar is full. You may need to add even more vinegar to guarantee that the oranges are covered.

2. Leave to instill for three to 4 weeks, the pressure of the vinegar, and also bottle for use thinned down in a variety of recipes.

Perfumed Herbal Vinegar

Technique: Recycling

This hand-made soap is an exceptional alternative to extreme shampoo, as it is excellent at both nurturing the hair and cleaning and also scalp. Vinegar is used as a rinse to be applied after washing with soap to smooth the hair shaft and bring back the acid mantle. I have made use of soap and also vinegar to clean my hair for numerous years, and once you get used to the slightly different feel, it is beneficial and much cheaper. You can make your very own scented herbal vinegars for use as a rinse or to include in cleansing items.

Base Contents

1 liter (1 3/4 pints) cider vinegar

Botanicals

50g (1 3/4 oz) lavender buds

50g (1 3/4 oz) increased petals

50g (1 3/4 oz) any other fresh or dried out natural herbs (optional).

Tools

Large Kilner container.

1. Place the lavender buds, increased flowers or any other fresh or dried out herbs you want to use right into a big jar, until it is one 3rd loaded. Pour a big container of cider vinegar to the top of the box, over the herbs or petals.

2. Leave the vinegar to instill in a warm, bright location for three weeks.

3. Strain off the natural herbs and either repeat for a more potent mixture or use directly away.

Using Your Vinegar Rinse.

Once you have made your vinegar mixture, you can maintain it in the restroom for washing; just put an inch of vinegar right into a container and leading it up with cozy water.

For another scent, you can add a couple of declines of essential oils, but the vinegar scent soon dissipates. Put over your head, massage therapy right into your hair and scalp for a couple of minutes and rinse afterward. Maintain your eyes near to prevent obtaining vinegar in them and view your step, as it can make the bathroom a little slippery!

Washing Shred

Method: Recycling.

If you find yourself stuck with only the soap around, it soon becomes a sensible concept to use it in as many methods as feasible! Making this washing powder is a brilliant way to conserve money, minimize product packaging, and lower your effect on the atmosphere. This is a straightforward recipe that can be made and kept in a completely dry cupboard.

Base Ingredients.

- 200g (7oz) soap.

- 100g (3½ oz) borax replacement - 100g (3½ oz) cleaning soda.

Botanicals.

- Twenty decreases of important lavender oil.

Tools

- Bowl.

- Cheese grater.

- Coffee grinder or mixer - Large container or container.

Herb Basics.

Eliminate limescale or soap residue and also add more scent to your washing by adding to the rinse cycle, a tablespoon(tbsp) of vinegar, and some quantity of essential oil.

1. Grate the soap into a bowl. Run your hands through the grated soap to break it right into smaller items. Leave the grated soap to completely dry for a couple of days grind in a mixer or coffee mill to minimize the dimension of the soap pieces.

2. Add the other dry active ingredients and also the vital lavender oil. Mix till thoroughly combined.

3. Decant the washing shred into a jar or container.

Multi-purpose Cleaning Spray.

Technique: Recycling.

Several home cleaning items are much harsher than a lot of home spills requirements. On top of that, they are pricey, use eco-unfriendly product packaging, and are typically made with rough chemicals.

This is a straightforward recipe that is used for essential cleansing, and it can be quickly modified if you want something more reliable.

You will need to load one spray bottle of cleaning spray.

Base Ingredients.

- 10g (1/4 oz) carefully grated soap - 5g (1/8 oz) bicarbonate of soft drink (baking soft drink).

- Hot filtered water.

Botanicals.

- Twenty declines of tea tree oil.

Tools

- Spray container.

- Cheese grater.

- Funnel.

- Spoon.

Organic Basics

All the vital ingredients used in this spray are safer to make use of in a home with family pets and children than shop-bought cleaning sprays.

1. Include the carefully grated soap to the spray container. Include the bicarbonate of soft drink, tea tree oil, and hot water through a channel.

2. Swish the container around gently to ensure that the soap and bicarbonate of soft drink liquifies. Once liquified, your spray is ready to make use of it!

Strategy Idea

Bear in mind to tremble the container before each use.

Creating Your Recipe

Crafting your own cold process soap recipe is much easier than you might think. Below we mention the few simple steps involved in formulating your personalized formulas.

1. First of all, choose your oils: You want to hold the unique characteristics of each oil in mind. As you are starting, it's a good idea to include olive oil, palm oil or vegetable shortening, and coconut oil. These three essential oils are going to give you the right lathering bar that solidifies well. As you become more conscious of how oils function independently of each other, you will deviate more from this set. Hold the olive oil and palm oil in relatively similar amounts, adding only half the volume of coconut oil.

2. Once you have selected your main base oils, you can choose your complimentary oils. Make a list of all the oils you use and the percentages in grams, or whatever the SAP map is weighing.

3. First, check the SAP map to find the SAP meaning for each oil you need.

4. Multiply the quantity of olive oil by 0.134 (SAP value)= the amount of lye used to saponify the olive oil in your recipe. Repeat the process for all five of the oils.

5. Next step, add all the quantities of lye required for each oil to determine the amount of lye needed for the final solution. You can recommend doing a lye discount or a supper fatting strategy, which effectively reduces the amount of lye necessary marginally. As a result, not all oils will be fully saponified, making certain oils more usable in moisturizers.

6. Calculate the amount of distilled water you need for your recipe. Generally, the amount of water you use will be about two to three times the amount of lye you use. The more water you make use of, the softer the soap becomes. If you want an excellent bar, you can double the amount of lye, for a lighter bar, you can try about three times the amount of lye. Using more water than this will make the soap very moist and not solidify. Using less water than this will result in "lye pockets," which are areas of lee that have not responded to the saponification cycle. Such pockets are substantial, undissolved lyes and may inflict chemical burns on the skin.

7. Eventually, choose any fragrances, colorants, or chemicals.

That's it, a few options and a few simple calculations are all you need to build your exclusive homemade sope. Have fun making your soap, and don't be afraid to experiment with it. If it does not work out as expected, you can always use it to make a beautiful, hand-milled soap.

ALL-NATURAL LIVING

Before the creation of cleaning agent, soap was used to clean the face and body, hair, clothing, meals and everything that cleaning agents are used for currently We are now becoming increasingly knowledgeable about the suspicious ingredients and chemicals found in detergents and also expanding in problem for the damage they are triggering us, both inside and to the globe at big. Plastic waste is loading the oceans and landfill, leaching chemicals right into the water systems, and impacting us all. This inspired me to begin making my very own. When you have the first collection of ingredients, creating your very own cleaning products, recipe washer tablet, and shampoos cost a fraction of the cost of shop-bought, and also you can re-use packaging to avoid waste. This section of the book considers the series of items that you can develop from your homemade soap and how to produce them.

Organic Soap Making

Many people who practice the art of homemade soap making do so as a pastime. A few of these enthusiasts who think in creating their final items from natural non-animal products, fall under the classification of natural soap making. These homemade products are made the same way industrial soaps are made, other than the fact that the ingredients are different, and the amount of the batches are naturally much less.

Organic soap making has ended up being popular among hobbyists with sensitive skin or those who do not want to use animal products in the making of their products. A lot of homemade soaps use tallow, or animal fats as one of the ingredients.

This procedure uses the hot process method of making soaps, however, and that suggests that caustic soda or lye need to be used to develop the soaps. This chemical is generally the only chemical found in the end product. It is an essential active ingredient used to protect the product's shelf life so that the soap can properly saponify. Other than this chemical, homemade soaps are natural.

Since the components are gentle and mild, homemade organic products typically give no adverse results towards those with delicate skin. If they are allergic to the natural product itself, the only opportunity a person may have of giving an allergic reaction is, for example, individuals who dislike nuts might not do well with natural soaps made with oil extracts from nuts.

When adopting organic soap making, soap makers use a variety of ingredients that offer the natural soaps a unique twist. For instance, dried herbs, beeswax, oatmeal, and other natural plant materials are used. Some argue that wax is an animal by-product. Still, other soap makers disregard this as nit-picking, particularly given that beeswax is a beautiful active ingredient, and usually produces an excellent soap.

CONCLUSION

Soap making, as it is known today, is a craft that has been happening for centuries. The processes have transformed a little, and now, we are lucky enough to be able to do it out of satisfaction instead of a requirement.

It is a great experience to attempt new points. If you haven't tried Do It Yourself homemade soap, it is ideal that you strive this intriguing hobby currently. We hope this book has been your helpful overview in losing light on the various corners of self-made soap and directed you on exactly how to begin, exactly how to continue and exactly how to develop visually attractive and beautifully smelling bars of soap that exfoliate or nurture your skin.

Don't be afraid to get innovative with brand-new ingredients, color scheme, layout, and decors. Soap making is much like food preparation. The possibilities are limitless. Establish your imagination cost-free to check out.

Soap making does not encourage being negligent, but it is a craft that can be taken pleasure in by a lot of people. The next step is to begin. If you do not have accessibility to or just can't wait for supplies from a soap making business or craft shop, then take a journey to your regional supermarket tonight and purchase a few soap-making recipes.

It is effortless to get started. Enjoy your soap making process as it is expected and be confident that you will discover ideas each step of the way.

www.ingramcontent.com/pod-product-compliance
Lightning Source LLC
Chambersburg PA
CBHW071829080526
44589CB00012B/961